THE GREEN BAY PACKERS ALL-TIME ALL-STARS

THE BEST PLAYERS AT EACH POSITION FOR THE GREEN AND GOLD

CHUCK CARLSON

LYONS
PRESS

Guilford, Connecticut

An imprint of The Rowman & Littlefield Publishing Group, Inc.
4501 Forbes Blvd., Ste. 200
Lanham, MD 20706
www.rowman.com

Distributed by NATIONAL BOOK NETWORK

British Library Cataloguing in Publication Information available

Library of Congress Cataloging-in-Publication Data

Names: Carlson, Chuck, 1957- author.
Title: The Green Bay Packers all-time all-stars : the best players at each
  position for the green and gold / Chuck Carlson.
Description: Guilford, Connecticut : Lyons Press, [2019] | Includes
  bibliographical references.
Identifiers: LCCN 2019021994 | ISBN 9781493041770 (paperback) | ISBN
  9781493041787 (ebook)
Subjects: LCSH: Green Bay Packers (Football team)—Biography. | Green Bay
  Packers (Football team)—History. | Football players—United
  States—Biography.
Classification: LCC GV956.G7 C3645 2019 | DDC 796.332/640977561—dc23
LC record available at https://lccn.loc.gov/2019021994

∞™ The paper used in this publication meets the minimum requirements of American National Standard for Information Sciences—Permanence of Paper for Printed Library Materials, ANSI/NISO Z39.48-1992.

CONTENTS

INTRODUCTION

They started with nothing, those first players who made up what would become the Green Bay Packers football team.

Yet from those meager beginnings, legends were born.

These first Packers were a bunch of mostly local guys, many of whom had played football in college, but some who had not. They were drawn together by their obsession with the violent, exhilarating, still relatively new sport of football that, only a decade or so earlier, was nearly legislated out of existence because it was considered by many to be too dangerous.

But that didn't stop these guys, who would do anything to play it.

It was 1919, a year after the end of the Great War, and America was learning just how strong and powerful it was becoming, The sport of football was the embodiment of that strength. It was a tough game played by tough guys and, more often than not, it was the toughest guys who won.

So, behind a young visionary, a group gathered in Green Bay, Wisconsin, a rugged paper mill town known mostly for its witheringly cold winters, to play the game they loved. And that's when, and that's where, the Green Bay Packers were born.

Sponsored, as everyone who knows anything about football knows (and many who don't), by the Indian Packing Company, they took the nickname of the company that kept them financially above water and functioning. Over time, the name "Packers" became synonymous with professional football.

This was the first edition of the Green Bay Packers, a team put together by a local kid, Earl Lambeau, known to everyone as "Curly," and George Calhoun, the sports editor of the local newspaper.

Lambeau had been something of a big shot on the high school football field at East High School in Green Bay. He went on to college, first at the University of Wisconsin (where he left after one year when the freshman football team was disbanded) and then to the University of Notre Dame, where George Gipp and Knute Rockne were already building their legends.

A bad case of tonsillitis forced Lambeau out of school and back to Green Bay, where he went to work as a shipping clerk at the Indian Packing Company.

But the desire to play football remained strong in Lambeau. So, along with Calhoun and $500 donated by the packing company, a new team was formed.

Ironically, Lambeau never wanted to name the new team "Packers." In fact, he never liked the name, but it made sense since the team was formed with the help of the packing company. And it was better than the name Calhoun had used in some early stories—"the Big Bay Blue Boys."

There was no National Football League yet but the roots were already forming, healthy and driving deep into the American consciousness. And while pro football was not necessarily born in Green Bay, it found its identity there. And there it has stayed.

In 1921 the Packers joined the American Professional Football Association, which had been formed in 1920 by another pro football visionary, George Halas, who created and coached a team in downstate Decatur, Illinois. The next year, that team moved to Chicago and eventually became the Bears.

But even in 1920, Halas had his issues with Green Bay and did not believe the team in this tiny community could compete in his new league.

After long, sometimes acrimonious, negotiations (What must it have been like to be in the talks between those two headstrong men?) it was agreed Green Bay could join.

In 1922 the APFA was renamed the National Football League, with teams mostly located in the Midwest (the Packers are the only franchise that has remained in its original location).

Over the decades the NFL would evolve, expand, and become the multibillion-dollar behemoth that it is today.

But that was for later. In 1919 the Packers were still just a collection of guys who loved the game. They would play any team anywhere because that's what made it so much fun.

The names of the players from that Packers team are mostly forgotten—except, of course, for Lambeau.

Indeed, that first Packers team featured a player named Rigney "Riggie" Dwyer, a star end who had been a local standout at Green Bay West High School. A veteran of World War I, during which he played football in France, he returned to join Lambeau with the Packers. But after the 1920 season he lost his right arm and leg while working in the railroad yards and his career was over.

That first Packers team also featured guys named Jim Coffeen and Milt Wilson, Wes Leaper and Kyle "Cowboy" Wheeler, Andy Muldoon and Henry "Tubby" Bero, and others whose names have faded from time and memory and history.

That first Packers team won 10 of its 11 games, losing only a season finale to the Beloit Fairies, 6–0, because, as Calhoun fulminated the next day in the sports pages of the *Press-Gazette*, "Capt. Lambeau's team was robbed of victory by referee Zabel of Beloit. This official penalized Green Bay three times after touchdowns, refusing to allow the score. The Packers were twice on the verge of leaving the field but decided to play it out."

There was no championship in 1919 because no such thing existed. There was no championship in 1920 either when the Packers rolled to another great season against mostly other Wisconsin teams, posting a 9-1-1 record.

With the formation of the APFA in 1920 and then the NFL two years after that, everything changed. It was no longer about local guys wanting to continue playing football; it was about finding the best players available and paying them to do the job.

It began with the signing in 1921 of future Packers Hall of Fame tackle Howard "Cub" Buck, who was paid the ungodly sum of $75 per game. In the years to follow, a litany of Pro Football Hall of Famers would play for the Packers and, in their own way, put their stamp on both the franchise and the NFL.

They included wide receiver Don Hutson, halfback Johnny "Blood" McNally, linemen Mike Michalske and Cal Hubbard, and, of course, Lambeau himself, the first great star for the franchise and one whose legacy still permeates to the point that, even today, no one hears that name without thinking of the team he created.

In their existence the Packers have enjoyed an almost embarrassment of riches in terms of all-star talent. Whatever the decade and no matter the success on the field, there have always been players who have been identified with the Packers.

Just consider Arnie Herber and Clarke Hinkle, Bart Starr and Jim Taylor, and Forrest Gregg, Jerry Kramer, and Willie Davis.

Keep looking and you'll find John Brockington and Paul Coffman, Don Majkowski and Tim Harris. It continued to Brett Favre, Reggie White, LeRoy Butler, and Ahman Green, and the list keeps going in more recent years with Charles Woodson, Clay Matthews, Greg Jennings, Donald Driver, and Aaron Rodgers.

As of 2018 there are 23 players enshrined in the Pro Football Hall of Fame who spent their prime years playing for the Packers. There is also one coach, Vince Lombardi, and one general manager, Ron Wolf. And down the road, more will follow.

And every player who puts on the uniform understands just how important that is and that they are playing for a franchise that has seen it all and done it all. They feel the history and the responsibility that goes with it.

Indeed, as Packers coach Mike Holmgren said when his team won the Super Bowl XXXI Lombardi Trophy after the 1996 season, as important as winning the trophy is for every team, it means more in Green Bay. Because, in a very real sense, it all started in Green Bay.

This is a book that will attempt to pick players at each position and anoint them Packers all-stars. It is, of course, an all-but-impossible endeavor, rather like a parent picking a favorite child. But it's an intriguing exercise nonetheless. And since this is such a subjective effort, by no means will everyone agree. Nor should they.

Still, it's fun to compare eras and athleticism and competition and decide, when push comes to shove, who are the 26 best players in Packers history. And, naturally, who is the best coach to lead that collection of all-stars.

So this is that effort to look at a remarkable history of success—and, yes, failure—and put together an all-star starting roster for the ages.

I hope you enjoy this journey back in time with a franchise that, in many ways, has defined what the NFL was, what it is, and what it could be in the future.

And while you'll recognize the names of these players and their exploits and accomplishments, it is almost as important to remember back to those players in 1919 when the game, and the world they lived in, was so very different.

Those early players never thought about Super Bowl rings or the riches of free agency or playing in a well-known cathedral of a stadium named after the guy they played with.

But make no mistake, the Green Bay Packers of 1919 are every bit as much a part of the team's history as the current edition.

So as the greats of Packers history are celebrated and revered, think back to guys like Orlo Wylie McLean and Gus Rosenow and Al Petoka from 1919, guys who played the game because they loved the game.

They weren't legends. But they were Packers. And, in the long and storied history of this franchise, maybe that's what matters most.

A Note on Players from Different Eras

This All-Star team will consist of 14 players on offense and 12 on defense. The punter will be included with the defense and the placekicker and kick returner with the offense. And there will be a head coach.

We are comparing different eras. No one expects the Packers' Super Bowl I championship team, with players like Bart Starr, Ray Nitschke, Willie Davis, and Max McGee, to compete with the Packers' Super Bowl XXXI victors of Brett Favre, Reggie White, Mark Chmura, and LeRoy Butler.

The point is to look at the players in the context of their time, place, and impact on the game they played, when they played it.

For example, there was no better wide receiver in the NFL of the 1930s and 1940s than Don Hutson and no better offensive lineman than Forrest Gregg in the 1960s. But times change and players are far different physically than they were decades ago.

We hope this book will be viewed in that way, knowing full well the game has changed—for both better and worse—in its long, turbulent history.

So let's get started and name a head coach for this bunch . . .

HEAD COACH

The Candidates

Earl "Curly" Lambeau
Vince Lombardi
Mike Holmgren

There was a now infamous poll conducted by the *Milwaukee Journal* in 1990 asking readers, and by extension Packers fans, who they believed was the best coach in team history. And the winner in that long-ago poll? Lindy Infante. Yes, Lindy Infante.

Perhaps that result shows how important winning was to Packers fans—especially in those days when winning was as rare as palm trees in Lambeau Field.

Lindy Infante, for all of you who have forgotten, was the Packers' head coach for four seasons, from 1988 to 1991. He had one winning season and no trips to the playoffs.

But that one season was indeed something special. Full of last-second comebacks and thrilling rallies, it was the season of the "Instant Replay" game when a last-second game-winning touchdown pass from Don Majkowski to Sterling Sharpe, at first negated by a penalty, was reversed by replay officials and led to a win over the hated Chicago Bears. To this day, the Bears media guide places an asterisk next to that result and Packers fans, on cue, say "Upon further review, the Bears still suck."

The Packers posted a 10-6 record in that 1989 season and, though they still missed the playoffs, 10 wins were enough for desperate Packers fans to cling to and to label Infante as the savior. Thus, in this rather less-than-scientific poll, they ignored Curly Lambeau and they brushed aside Vince Lombardi and they hailed Infante as the franchise's greatest coach in history.

Fortunately, most Packers fans look upon that ancient statement of faith as a bout of temporary insanity brought on by a promising, but short-lived, excursion back to the promised land.

Great coaches, especially for a franchise as popular as the Packers, are great all the time—not for one season. They set a tone, a standard, a way their players play the game that has their fingerprints all over it.

They attain success and they maintain it through all circumstances—whether it's injuries or bad luck or circumstances that are sometimes within their control, but often are not.

So it is with our three candidates for the man who will coach our all-star team. Lindy Infante, sadly, did not make the cut.

Still, let's briefly go back to his mostly forgettable four-year tenure with the Packers because it is critical to what happened before his arrival and what would happen in the future.

Now, Packers fans back in the late 1980s did not live in a vacuum, but they did live in a time when the words "success" and "Packers" did not reside in the same sentence. Indeed, it had been an awful time to root for the team. Mediocrity hung over the franchise like a fog, penetrating everything and everyone.

Since the Packers had last won a world title, 20 very long seasons before, it had been almost abject disappointment for the once proud franchise. Indeed, the image of the legendary Vince Lombardi being carried off the Orange Bowl field, after his Packers had beaten the Oakland Raiders in the second Super Bowl, seemed almost like a dream to most Packers fans.

An ailing and exhausted Lombardi had stepped away as head coach prior to the 1968 season, and since then four coaches had managed to generate just three winning seasons and two playoff berths.

In the meantime, playing in Green Bay meant playing in cold mediocrity. In fact, several players, most famously future Packer Reggie White, relayed how coaches of other teams threatened players who weren't performing with a trade to Green Bay.

Phil Bengtson, Lombardi's loyal defensive coordinator and heir apparent, was saddled with a broken and aging team and managed a 20-21-1 record in three seasons. Not bad anywhere else but thoroughly unacceptable in Green Bay.

Dan Devine came to the Packers from the storied University of Notre Dame and lasted four seasons, finishing with a 25-27-2 mark that included one playoff berth. He headed back to the college ranks.

Legendary Packers quarterback Bart Starr took over after that and lasted a remarkable eight seasons despite a 52-76-3 mark that featured one playoff trip.

But it was already becoming something less than a badge of honor to play for the Packers. In fact, in 1980, when the Packers drafted Penn State defensive tackle Bruce Clark, a player the Packers knew could fill a major void on defense and who would likely be penciled in as a starter right away, Clark did the unthinkable.

Instead of going on to fame and fortune in the NFL, Clark signed with the Toronto Argonauts of the Canadian Football League. It was a slap in the face not only to the NFL, but especially to the Packers—another sign that players would play anywhere other than Green Bay.

"No one goes to Canada to play," Packers quarterback Lynn Dickey recalled in a story in the *Milwaukee Journal Sentinel*. "But he did."

But the Packers absorbed the embarrassment and moved on. Clark played two seasons in Canada, then signed with the New Orleans Saints (who surrendered a first-round draft pick to the Packers in exchange) and later the Kansas City Chiefs. He played 10 seasons and never regretted his decision to escape Green Bay.

Another Packer from the pantheon, Hall of Fame tackle Forrest Gregg, came in next and left after four seasons with a 25-37-1 mark. Worse, he built a Packers team known for its raucous, undisciplined play. It was a team of misfits and underachievers whose names appeared as often in the police blotter as the sports pages.

If there was a rock bottom in the history of the Green Bay Packers, the Gregg era may well have been it. Not only was the franchise considered a joke by the rest of the NFL, worst of all, it was considered irrelevant.

So when a guy named Lindy Infante, who had performed well as offensive coordinator of the Cleveland Browns, was hired as the team's latest head coach in 1988, not much was expected.

In fact, Infante wasn't even the Packers' first choice, moving up the ladder when their chosen candidate, Michigan State head coach George Perles, first agreed to a deal with Green Bay and then backed out at the last minute. Into the breach stepped Infante, who had longed to be a head coach and would view the Packers position as the opportunity of a lifetime.

But Infante had no better success his first year than any of those coaches who preceded him. The Packers slogged to a 4-12 record, notable mostly for the fact that they went through four field goal kickers and never did find one who could do the job.

But in 1989 everything changed. These Packers played with abandon and joy and a healthy dose of good fortune. Under Infante's leadership, and the play of a swashbuckling quarterback named Don Majkowski, Green Bay won 10 games for the first time since 1972 and though they missed the playoffs, fans were giddy with excitement and anticipation for what the future might hold.

But it didn't last. Seeing his value to the team, Majkowski decided to hold out of training camp the following season, awaiting a better contract. He finally ended his holdout but the damage had been done.

Majkowski was awful, then injured, and a cast of quarterbacks including Anthony Dilweg and Blair Kiel tried to fill in with little success. A 6-10 season resulted and the next year, it was a 4-12 monstrosity.

By that stage, long-suffering team president Bob Harlan, who had held various jobs with the team over 20 years and had yearned for the day his Packers would turn the corner, had finally had enough.

He hired former New York Jets executive Ron Wolf to take over as general manager and gave him the awesome responsibilities not offered to a Packers GM since Vince Lombardi.

"Do what you need to do," Harlan told Wolf. "But fix this."

That was 1992.

And much has changed.

But let's be clear. In the long and sometimes storied history of Packers head coaches, there are really only three who merit consideration as candidates for the best of all time.

These three changed the game, changed the fortunes of the Packers, and changed a franchise in their special way.

Earl "Curly" Lambeau

Simply put, Lambeau is the reason Green Bay is an NFL city. It probably never should have happened and in another time and another circumstance, it probably would not have.

But it did. And Green Bay continues to be a flagship NFL franchise, with fans across the globe and a reputation that goes far beyond what occurs on the football field.

It was the smallest city in the American Professional Football Association when it joined that league in 1921, and it remains the smallest city today in an NFL that boasts two teams in New York and Los Angeles as well as high-profile franchises in Dallas, Chicago, Houston, Philadelphia, and nearly every other metropolis in America.

Lambeau was a terrific player for the early Packers, playing halfback in the vaunted single-wing offense. But he was crucial not only in the team's formation, but in keeping it alive in the early days when the team struggled financially.

Lambeau was more than a player and more than a coach—he was a shrewd marketer, a solid businessman, and an excellent

Curly Lambeau in 1940
WIKIMEDIA COMMONS

judge of football talent. And, of course, when he took over as head coach, he helped expand and revolutionize the game.

For example, along with a few other pioneers of the era, he understood how important the forward pass would become to the game. And he used it with often devastating results.

He coached the Packers for their first 30 years and they were three decades in which the Packers saw everything—reaching the pinnacle of success and winning championships, and later being nearly driven out of business and needing mass public support and infusions of cash to stay alive.

Still, his teams would revolutionize football and were at the forefront of innovation, developing the passing game and designing the first pass patterns.

He was Green Bay's first general manager and he brought in players like Hall of Famers Don Hutson, Johnny McNally, and Clarke Hinkle. His teams were the first to fly to away games, and he learned early that training camps were important to get his teams ready for a season.

From 1920 (when Lambeau officially became player/coach), his Packers won six championships and they experienced just three losing seasons, two coming in his final two years with the team when the relationship between Lambeau and the Packers' board of directors had shattered beyond repair.

But when it all ended after the 1949 season, Lambeau had long ago established himself as an NFL icon. His 209 wins as Packers coach will never be touched and will always be inextricably linked to his influence on the game.

Still, all good things end. And so it was with Lambeau and his relationship with the Packers organization.

He was innovative and smart and driven; no one could deny that. Lambeau had turned the Packers into a powerhouse of the fledgling NFL and put little Green Bay on the professional sports map.

And because he had done it all, and more, Lambeau developed a reputation among many of his players as egotistical and stubborn. These were descriptions Lambeau did nothing to refute.

One of his early stars, back Clarke Hinkle, said it simply on Packers.com: "I never liked him and I never really respected him either. But he was paying me and I gave him a thousand percent every time I played football for him."

And, in truth, that's all Lambeau demanded.

But the issues grew deeper as the years went by. It had been decided early on in the franchise's creation that the Packers would be run by an executive committee with the power to oversee the financial health of the team. Personnel issues? That was the job of the general manager, and the general manager was Lambeau.

And for years, the Packers thrived on the field. But after they beat the New York Giants for the 1944 NFL championship, signs of trouble began to show up.

Subpar (but still winning) seasons were recorded over the next three years, which was cause enough for concern. But Lambeau was making decisions that puzzled and at times infuriated the Packers' increasingly uncomfortable board of directors.

For example, in 1946 he convinced the executive committee to spend $25,000 on the infamous Rockwood Lodge, a getaway 17 miles outside Green Bay that Lambeau believed would provide players with a chance to train and regroup away from the prying eyes of Packers fans.

Instead, Packers officials saw it as a way for Lambeau to get away from having to answer their questions. Worse, it alienated Packers fans, who viewed it as a way for players to separate from the fans who had been so loyal over the years.

On the personal front, Lambeau had gone through a very public and very nasty divorce from his first wife and was now remarried and spending more time in California with his new wife than in Green Bay.

Meanwhile, the performance on the field continued to spiral out of control. A 3-9 record in 1948 was the worst in the proud franchise's history until 1949, when they fell to 2-10.

Early that season, Lambeau relinquished full-time control as head coach to a trio of assistant coaches so he could concentrate on his GM duties. But the triumvirate of Bob Snyder, Tom Stidham, and Charley Brock made little difference.

The proverbial handwriting was on the wall for the Packers and the franchise's founding father.

Offered a new two-year contract after the 1949 season, Lambeau delayed signing it. Finally on January 30, 1950, citing "dangerous disunity of purpose within the corporation," Lambeau resigned and accepted the position of vice president and head coach of the Chicago Cardinals.

It was over. The Green Bay native who brought professional football to the little city, kept it there, and, oh yes, built a powerhouse, was out—jumping from the plane before he was pushed, though just barely.

But Green Bay never forgot Curly Lambeau and Curly Lambeau never forgot Green Bay. Two miserable seasons with the Cardinals led to his dismissal, and they were followed by two more awful seasons as head coach of the Washington Redskins, where he was also fired.

Lambeau stepped away from coaching after that but maintained relationships in the Green Bay area. On June 1, 1965, he was at his summer home in Sturgeon Bay, a holiday enclave north of Green Bay, when he suffered a heart attack and died at age 67.

If Lambeau's fortunes as a head coach had swooned after leaving the Packers, the Packers had fared no better since Lambeau left.

Since his last season in Green Bay in 1949, six coaches over nine seasons had failed to produce a winning season. A new guy, a former offensive coordinator of the New York Giants named Vince Lombardi, had taken over in 1959 and turned the Packers' fortunes around, going to three straight NFL title games and winning the last two, in 1961 and 1962.

Now it was the opening game of the 1965 season (the Packers would beat the Cleveland Browns to win another title at the end of that season, too), and it was time to let bygones be bygones.

In honor of everything Lambeau had done for the Packers, it was decided that City Stadium would be renamed Lambeau Field. And while Lombardi was publicly in favor of the decision, deep down he seethed. He saw Lambeau as a womanizer whose runaway ego had shattered the franchise for years.

But Lambeau Field still stands, perhaps one of the most recognizable sports venues in the world.

And Lambeau would look on and smile.

Lambeau was named to the NFL's All-Decade Team for the 1920s and was inducted into the Pro Football Hall of Fame in 1963.

And at his induction ceremony, his great rival, George Halas of the Chicago Bears, paid Lambeau the ultimate compliment.

"He was such a great builder in our league," Halas said. "Without him, pro football simply wouldn't exist as it does now."

VINCE LOMBARDI

What is there left to say about this man? Dozens of books have been written about him and his approach to football and life. A play has been written about him. There is a statue of him at

Vince Lombardi and his quarterback, Bart Starr

Lambeau Field. A major road named for him runs past Lambeau Field. A school in Green Bay is named after him. His home, a mile from the stadium, remains something of a sacred site as fans drive past just to look.

And, of course, the Super Bowl trophy, what every NFL team aspires to claim, is named after him.

Not only is the name Lombardi synonymous with the Green Bay Packers, but it is somehow almost sacrilege not to link the two, as if there is not one without the other.

But, of course, there was and now Vince Lombardi exists only in myth and rumor and the memory of those who once played for him as well as in old newsreels that tell only a fraction of the story of this remarkable, flawed man.

He was a saint and a demon and a legend who always demanded perfection in himself and his players—knowing full well he, and they, would never find it. That's what he told his new team in their first meeting, and it reverberated with many of them.

Yet he brought out the best in all his players through a combination of intimidation, fear, and grudging respect. Many of his players loved him for it; just as many hated him. But all played hard for the "old man" and none of them ever forgot the lessons he taught them.

"Vince Lombardi made me the man I am," Hall of Fame guard Jerry Kramer has said often. "I owe everything to him."

As the decades have gone by, the view of Vince Lombardi has hardened into concrete. He is considered by many the greatest coach in NFL history and by just as many as a coach who used intimidation and degradation to get the job done.

But no one argued with the results.

In his nine seasons with the Packers, he posted a 98-30-4 record, still the best in team history. His 1960 team reached the franchise's first NFL Championship Game since 1944 but fell to the Philadelphia Eagles.

Afterward he famously told his disconsolate team they would never lose another championship game as long as he was head coach. And they didn't—winning titles in 1961, 1962, 1965, 1966, and 1967 and establishing the Packers as the gold standard of the NFL at a time when the league was soaring in popularity.

Lombardi coached with a combination of intimidation, rage, and fear. He was a smart tactician but a better motivator, knowing which players to push to their limits and which players to pull back on. And the players knew it, too.

Indeed, Lombardi's methods, as effective and forceful as they were in the 1960s, would likely not be tolerated in today's NFL and, perhaps, that's why his name continues to reverberate all these decades later.

Lombardi knew his reputation and he played it to the fullest and, as a result, it brought out the best in his players. He didn't care if they hated him or loved him; he just wanted them to give every ounce of energy they could.

It's also why Lombardi established early that he would accept nothing else.

Indeed, mere weeks after accepting the head coaching position in 1959, Lombardi sent a letter to his star halfback, Paul Hornung, telling him what was expected of him in terms of his weight and preparation for training camp.

Some players might have been infuriated by Lombardi's pointed remarks, but not Hornung. Believing he'd been criminally underused in his first three seasons with the Packers, he loved the fact that the new coach had made it clear he would make him the focal point of the offense.

The two men went on to enjoy a close, fractious, successful partnership.

The stories about Lombardi have reached legendary status and many of them never even occurred. For example, the story of All-Pro center Jim Ringo, who hired an agent to negotiate his contract (as few players did back then) and demanded a raise prior to the start of the 1964 season.

The story goes that Lombardi excused himself from the meeting, came back a few minutes later, and said, "Congratulations, Jim, you've been traded to the Philadelphia Eagles."

It was a great story and one that Lombardi did nothing to refute. In truth, though, Ringo had wanted a trade anyway, preferably to the Eagles, since Philadelphia was home to him.

But Lombardi saw the benefit of a good story because he was concerned about the growing power of agents in pro football. This was his statement that coaches still made the final decisions.

One story that was true was relayed by former center Bill Curry, who played for the Packers in 1965 and 1966. A cerebral, quiet guy who had played his college football at Georgia Tech, he was not used to the verbal tsunamis he received on an almost daily basis from Lombardi—and he did not understand or appreciate them.

In 1967 he was left unprotected in the expansion draft and was selected by the New Orleans Saints, who a month later traded him to the Baltimore Colts.

Prior to Super Bowl III, which saw the New York Jets upset the heavily favored Colts, Curry, now the Colts' starting center, went off to reporters about how much he enjoyed playing for

Baltimore coach Don Shula because he treated his players like men.

Then, at a charity banquet in 1969, Lombardi saw Curry and his former player didn't know what to expect. That's when Lombardi held out his hand and greeted Curry as a long-lost son.

The next year, as Lombardi lay dying in his hospital room, Curry visited his old coach and apologized for what he had said about him. Lombardi forgave him and Curry never forgot.

It was yet another side to a man everyone thought they knew but whom no one really understood.

As good a coach as Lombardi was for the first eight years of his career in Green Bay, perhaps his greatest coaching job came in 1967 as his aging and injured Packers tried to accomplish what no other team had in NFL history—winning three straight league titles.

But it would not be easy.

Lombardi, himself exhausted and ill, saw that these Packers were in a similar state. But they battled through injuries and inconsistency and reached the NFL Championship Game against the young, confident, and very talented Dallas Cowboys.

They would meet on December 31, 1967, with the winner playing the AFL champion in Super Bowl II. The game would be played at Lambeau Field in the kind of ghastly cold weather that required a nickname so history would remember it. And forever and always, this game would be known as the "Ice Bowl."

For four quarters, the two battered teams slammed away at each other—until the final seconds, when the Packers cobbled together a drive that led to the winning touchdown.

The details have been recorded everywhere, and more than 50 years later there is nothing about the game football fans do not know.

That was Lombardi's last home game as the Packers' head coach. Two weeks later, his team dispatched the AFL's Oakland Raiders and won their second straight Super Bowl. And the iconic photo of Jerry Kramer carrying Lombardi off the field is as poignant now as it was then.

Mere weeks later, ready for a break and a new challenge, Lombardi relinquished his head coaching duties to his long-time defensive coordinator, Phil Bengtson. Lombardi would slip away and concentrate on his duties as the Packers' general manager.

But he was a head coach and always would be. His one season as Green Bay GM was agony. He watched his aging team stumble on the field. He watched it make mistakes that would have been unheard of in years past. He watched Bengtson go in directions he never would have. And he tried to keep his distance.

He had his private booth high above Lambeau Field soundproofed so that on game days the press who resided next door would not hear him raging at what he was watching on the field. Everyone who knew Lombardi realized how miserable and helpless he looked and felt.

Lombardi knew it, too, and after the 1968 season (the Packers' first losing season since 1958, a year before Lombardi arrived), he resigned as GM to take over as head coach and general manager of another struggling franchise, the Washington Redskins.

His one season in Washington was a success as he led to the Redskins to a 7-5-2 record, their first winning mark since 1955.

But it would not last. Weeks before the start of the 1970 season Lombardi was diagnosed with colon cancer and, despite surgery, the seemingly indestructible man would not survive.

Lombardi died on September 3, 1970, at the age of 57 and more than 3,500 mourners attended his funeral in his native New York City. Three of his favorite Packers players—Willie Davis, Bart Starr, and Paul Hornung—served as pallbearers.

Three days after the funeral, NFL commissioner Pete Rozelle announced that the trophy presented to the Super Bowl champion would be named for Lombardi.

And his name has lived on, the thunderous symbol of an era in professional football that will never be seen again.

MIKE HOLMGREN

Handed virtually total control to remake the Green Bay Packers in 1992, Ron Wolf's first and second decisions could arguably be called the smartest of his entire tenure.

The first was to fire the hopelessly overmatched Lindy Infante after four mostly pointless seasons as head coach. The second was to immediately go after the hottest young assistant coach in the NFL and convince him Green Bay was the place for him to excel.

Mike Holmgren had already made a name for himself as quarterbacks coach for the best team of the decade, the San Francisco 49ers. Learning at the side of the 49ers' innovative head coach, Bill Walsh, Holmgren absorbed the tiniest details of the so-called West Coast Offense, which relied on a short, precise passing game to gain yardage.

Holmgren felt he was ready to be a head coach. In the spring of 1992, he was the hot commodity and his services were

Mike Holmgren

already being sought by the Miami Dolphins and New York Jets.

In Green Bay, all Wolf had to sell Holmgren on was his guarantee that he would remake the Packers into exciting, relevant, consistent winners.

Holmgren could not resist that challenge.

He accepted Green Bay's offer and prepared to put his fingerprints all over the new Packers. Then, just a few days into his employment, Wolf dropped a bomb.

"I'm going to trade our No. 1 draft pick for Brett Favre," the GM told Holmgren. "What do you think?"

"What was I going to say?" Holmgren said later.

He already had a quarterback in Don Majkowski that he knew he could work with, but he also knew that Majkowski, by then, was a fully formed product who had already played extensively in the NFL—indeed, he'd already been to a Pro Bowl.

Holmgren could try to break habits that Majkowski had developed and attempt to create the kind of quarterback Holmgren knew he'd need if he was to be successful in Green Bay.

But, deep down, he knew that wasn't going to happen.

He was intrigued by Favre, a quarterback in his second season who was smoldering on the bench in Atlanta and whom Holmgren admits he knew little about until he came to Green Bay in this unfathomable trade. But Holmgren had faith that Wolf knew what he was doing.

Nevertheless, Majkowski got the start in Holmgren's first NFL game as a head coach, and he was every bit the quarterback Holmgren had expected—and feared.

The West Coast Offense, which relied on precision timing and ball location, wasn't his strong suit. In an overtime loss to the Minnesota Vikings, Majkowski threw for 189 yards and two touchdowns. Not bad. But he was also intercepted once and sacked six times—two statistics that would always drive Holmgren crazy.

In the second game, a disastrous 31–3 loss to the Tampa Bay Buccaneers, Holmgren pulled the ineffective Majkowski and gave Favre a look.

As the history of the Packers has so often recorded, Favre's first pass was tipped and caught—by himself. And it only got worse.

Favre and Majkowski combined to throw for just 148 yards and were sacked six times. Both were also intercepted once.

"I was beginning to think I'd be the first head coach to be fired before I won a game," Holmgren recalled. "It was awful."

And then it all changed.

Again, Packers fans can recall precisely where they were and what they were doing when, in game three against the Cincinnati Bengals, Majkowski was injured and had to depart in favor of Favre.

Favre was all over the map, calling formations and plays that did not exist and testing Holmgren's infamous temper. But Wolf was right: this kid was special. He was a winner with a wondrous, infectious, child-like love of football that was rarely seen in the buttoned-down NFL.

His last-second touchdown pass beat the Bengals, and for the next 15 years he was Green Bay's starting quarterback. And on that day, Favre and Holmgren formed a partnership built on trust, conflict, paranoia, and, yes, love.

"He's the best coach I ever had," Favre said in his Hall of Fame induction speech in 2016. "I wouldn't have been the quarterback I became without him."

Said Holmgren at a speech honoring Favre, "I told Brett that first year that we were joined at the hip and that we would fail or succeed together. He's like the son I never had."

So the pieces to the Packers' revival were in place with Wolf as general manager, Holmgren as head coach, and Favre as quarterback.

Holmgren's teams got steadily better, making believers out of many who never thought the Packers would be relevant in the NFL again.

In 1995 the Packers went back to Holmgren's hometown of San Francisco and beat his former team, the 49ers, in the NFC playoffs. That earned them a trip to the NFC Championship, where they were beaten by the toughest kids on the block at the time, the Dallas Cowboys.

But in defeat Holmgren took a page from the Lombardi gospel. On the plane ride home, Holmgren told his team they would be back and to prepare for what it was going to feel like to go to the Super Bowl.

And so it was.

In January 1997 the Packers rolled over the Carolina Panthers in frigid Lambeau Field to claim the NFC title. On the sidelines stood the architect, Ron Wolf, laughing and crying at the same time.

"This feels better than I ever imagined," he said.

Two weeks later, the Packers claimed their first Super Bowl title in 30 years, beating the New England Patriots. And afterward, in an emotional speech to his team, Holmgren, holding the Lombardi Trophy, told his players, "As important as this is to every other team in the league, this means more to us."

The Packers returned to the Super Bowl the following season with what many observers believed was an even better team than the '96 edition.

But being the hunted was a new position for the Packers, and the Denver Broncos upset the heavily favored Packers. More to the point, both Holmgren and Favre came under criticism for their performances.

In 1998 the Packers continued in their role as one of the NFC's powerhouses. But something had changed.

A new power was rising, and in their own division. With a dynamic offense and a dominating defense, the Minnesota Vikings beat the Packers twice that season. Worse, a power struggle was developing between Wolf and Holmgren that would eventually fracture the team.

Holmgren was ready for more responsibility and felt he could handle the dual role of general manager and head coach. But Wolf, who had built the Packers into perhaps the new gold standard of how an NFL franchise should run, wasn't ready to cede control.

All season, the controversy bubbled just below the surface and some critics saw Green Bay's less-than-inspired play as a by-product of Holmgren's determination to spread his wings.

It culminated in a remarkable display during a November game at Lambeau Field against the hapless Philadelphia Eagles. The Packers had played poorly in the first half and led just 10–6 at halftime. As the team headed to the locker room, boos rained down—an unusual occurrence, to say the least.

As Holmgren, already furious by the team's showing, passed by the stands, one fan told him to get his head in the game and stop worrying about his future.

That's all it took.

Holmgren's famous temper ignited and he headed toward the stands to find the fan. He was stopped before he got close, but it was a dramatic sign that the good old days were done.

As the Packers prepared for their first-round playoff game in San Francisco, rumors swirled that Holmgren would replace his old friend and former Packers quarterbacks coach, Steve Mariucci, as the 49ers head coach.

All sides denied it, but the signs were obvious something would happen.

In the end the Packers lost a heartbreaker to the 49ers, and not even a week later Holmgren resigned to take over as executive vice president/general manager and head coach of the Seattle Seahawks.

He would go on to a successful 10-year career with the Seahawks, where he'd post a 90-80 record and win five division titles.

His absence in Green Bay would be felt for years. Convinced that the Packers needed a different type of coach, Wolf hired hard-nosed Ray Rhodes as Holmgren's replacement. He lasted one season.

Mike Sherman came on board after that, and when Wolf stunned everyone prior to the 2001 season with his decision to retire, Sherman assumed the twin roles Holmgren had always sought.

Would Holmgren have waited two more seasons for that opportunity he coveted so much? No one really knows, but chances are slim he could have, or would have, waited. Time is a factor in the NFL and opportunity waits for no one. Holmgren had the chance, and a hefty salary bump, from the Seahawks, and nothing was likely to stop him.

In the end, Sherman struggled doing the two rigorous jobs and lost the GM role to Ted Thompson in 2005. Holmgren, for his part, also struggled doing both jobs in Seattle and was replaced as Seahawks GM after the 2002 season.

Ironically, Holmgren enjoyed his greatest success in Seattle after he was relieved as GM, taking the Seahawks to four straight NFC West titles and a trip to the Super Bowl. He was fired after the 2008 season and a year later became general manager of the Cleveland Browns, where he stepped down after the 2012 season.

Mike Holmgren took over the Packers at a key time in their existence and his contributions will never be forgotten. He was the right combination of football mastermind and psychologist. He knew how to work in the Green Bay community, where coaches and players alike were expected, if not to make the community their home, to at least understand the symbiotic relationship between the team and the people who lived there.

Holmgren always liked to tell the story about an old lady in the grocery store. He had just started as head coach and expectations among fans were reasonably high for the new guy from San Francisco, which was so far removed socially, culturally, and economically from Green Bay that Holmgren may as well have flown in from Neptune.

Holmgren recalls the elderly lady looking at him in the store and, eventually, striding up to him.

"She looked at me and said, 'Kick some butt, California,'" Holmgren recalled.

He always got a good laugh, and whether the story was true or not was hardly the issue. Holmgren had an intrinsic, gut-level feel for how much these fans wanted and needed the

Packers to be good again. And he knew early on that any way he could convey his devotion to that goal was one more step in the right direction.

And, oh yes, he posted an 84-42 record in his seven seasons, taking the Packers to the playoffs (and two Super Bowls) in the final six years.

His .667 winning percentage is third-best in team history and, more important, he was the right coach at the right time for a franchise that was desperate for anything positive.

AND THE WINNER IS . . .

It would seem to be an easy decision, but look at each coach and his accomplishments and, just maybe, it's not so simple after all.

Green Bay native Curly Lambeau created the team that would become the Packers and, quite simply, he was one of the architects of what would become the National Football League. He coached the team for its first 31 seasons, won six NFL titles, and created what became a worldwide fan base.

Vince Lombardi was Vince Lombardi. A mercurial former offensive coordinator from the New York Giants whom few had heard of in 1959, he was reluctant to take the job at first. But, eventually, understanding the opportunity that it presented, he roared into town and changed the culture of that town and of its franchise. Tough and demanding, he made the players believe in his system and, by extension, they believed in themselves. The result was five NFL championships in his nine seasons and a spot in the NFL pantheon with precious few members.

Mike Holmgren, like Lombardi, took over a team that had lost faith in itself and its future and restored it through a new way of coaching. His teams were exciting and disciplined and fun to watch. And they were very good. His relationship with Brett Favre is well known, but what isn't quite so well known is how much all his players over the years respected him. In seven seasons his team qualified for the playoffs six times, won three division titles and two conference titles, and reached the Super Bowl in back-to-back seasons.

For this team, discipline and organization are paramount. And while every coach demands his players play the game the right way, the best at this, perhaps in league history, was Lombardi.

So, because of his reputation, success, and approach, the coach of our team, in a closer vote than expected, is **Vince Lombardi**.

COACHES WHO DID NOT MAKE THE CUT

Poor **Mike McCarthy**. He was a fine coach for the Packers who never got the credit and, perhaps worse, the respect he deserved. McCarthy had the second-longest tenure as the team's head coach in history, behind only Curly Lambeau. But he never quite made it through his 12th season. After a shattering home loss to the hapless Arizona Cardinals in November 2018, McCarthy was called upstairs and fired with four games left in a season spinning out of control.

His teams were always competitive, sometimes exciting, and often puzzling and, among his critics, they never excelled in the way many had hoped, especially with a Hall of Fame quarterback-in-waiting named Aaron Rodgers. Indeed, it was believed McCarthy was finally done in when it became clear Rodgers no longer felt McCarthy had control of the offense. Still, his teams won one Super Bowl (2010), but through mistakes or bad luck or bad execution, three other opportunities to reach the Super Bowl slipped away. And, in the end, winning was what mattered. His last two seasons in Green Bay resulted in sub-.500 marks and, even with a long leash and nearly inexhaustible patience from the front office, it was time for him to go.

McCarthy finished with a 125-77-2 (62 percent) record, and those 125 wins are second in team history only to Lambeau, who won 209 games.

Mike Sherman took over as Green Bay's head coach in 2000 after a turbulent 1999 season under Ray Rhodes, who was fired after just one season. Sherman went on to coach the Packers for six seasons, through 2005, and from 2000 to 2004 his winning percentage of .663 (53-27) was second only to Lombardi. But a 4-12 record in 2005 and a battle with new general manager Ted Thompson made it clear it was time for him to move on. He went on to become an assistant coach with the Houston Texans and Miami Dolphins and was also a collegiate head coach at Texas A&M. He even backed away from the rigors of the high-stakes and high-pressure world of college and pro football and coached at the high school level in his native Massachusetts for two years. But he returned to the pro game in 2018 and is now coaching with the Montreal Alouettes in the Canadian Football League.

Let's even put in a good word for **Bart Starr**, if only for his longevity and dedication to a franchise for which he gave so much and which gave so much to him. Starr had no head coaching experience of any kind when he stepped in to replace Dan Devine in 1975. He went on to coach the Packers for nine seasons, the fourth-longest tenure in team history, and posted a 53-77-3 record that included one playoff appearance. Most coaches, even then, would not have been given that kind of time to turn a team around. But because it was Bart Starr, there was always a reason to give him one more shot. It often wasn't a pleasant experience for Starr, and in later years he politely declined to go into much detail about his time on the sidelines. But he gave it everything he had and remains a beloved Packers icon.

Offense

QUARTERBACK

The Candidates

Bart Starr
Brett Favre
Aaron Rodgers

For the past two decades, most of the National Football League has looked longingly at the Green Bay Packers and their ridiculously talented, and stable, quarterback situation.

Consider that since Brett Favre stepped on the field on that September afternoon in 1992, only six players have started under center for the Packers—Brett Favre, Aaron Rodgers, Matt Flynn, Seneca Wallace, Scott Tolzien, and Brett Hundley.

And, oh yes, those first two? One is in the Pro Football Hall of Fame, and the other will join him a few years after he retires.

For some context, Hundley started nine games of the 2017 season after Rodgers broke his collarbone. He was so effective, he was traded prior to the start of the 2018 season.

In 2013 the Packers scrambled to find anyone to play quarterback after Rodgers broke his other collarbone. Wallace got the call to start the next game and lasted exactly one series when, as he scrambled away from defenders, he suffered a season-ending groin injury.

He was replaced by a thoroughly likable but completely overmatched Scott Tolzien, who lasted two games before he was replaced by Matt Flynn, who had returned to Green Bay after unsuccessful stops in Oakland and Seattle. Flynn lasted four games before Rodgers finally returned.

That was what counted as quarterback chaos in Green Bay. Now, consider other teams.

The Chicago Bears, since that same 1992 time frame, have given the starting assignment to 31 quarterbacks. Since returning to the NFL in 1999, the Cleveland Browns can count 30 starting quarterbacks. The Minnesota Vikings, since 1992, have had 27 quarterbacks. The Washington Redskins? Since 1992, 25 starters. Since Hall of Famer Dan Marino retired in 1999, the Miami Dolphins have started 19 different quarterbacks.

You get the idea.

Meanwhile, life has rolled on merrily and with relatively little angst in Green Bay. Brett Favre from 1992 to 2007. Aaron Rodgers from 2008 until at least 2018. And before that, there was Bart Starr, who played from 1957 to 1972, and when he was hurt there was the reliable Zeke Bratkowski.

The Packers have been fortunate to seemingly have a quality quarterback ready to step in when needed. There may be issues on defense or wide receiver or with coaching, but the key position on the football field, quarterback, has gone through little trauma in the NFL's smallest city.

Smart and tough and talented—stories have reverberated down the ages about how Packers quarterbacks have thrived.

There was Vince Lombardi and Bart Starr talking about perhaps the most important play of their careers.

There were 16 seconds remaining in the NFL Championship Game on December 31, 1967. The Packers had the ball on the Dallas Cowboys' 1-yard line on a literally frozen Lambeau Field. Time for one more play. If they scored, the Packers would win, but if they failed, there was no time for another play.

The veteran, savvy Starr called time-out and went to the sideline to talk over a final play with Lombardi. Seconds earlier Lombardi had asked his one-time star halfback Paul Hornung what play to run. He had no answers. (Hornung had been selected by the New Orleans Saints the previous season in the expansion draft but retired due to a neck injury. He was invited by Lombardi to stand on the sidelines for the game.)

The unflappable Starr approached the frenetic Lombardi and suggested a quarterback sneak.

Lombardi looked at him and said, in words that every Packers fan remembers, "Well, run the damn thing and let's get out of here."

Starr did, scoring one of the most famous touchdowns in NFL history, and the game known as the "Ice Bowl" remains one of the great images in American sports.

Then there was Brett Favre.

At a critical juncture of the Packers' 1996 NFC Championship Game against the Carolina Panthers on a frigid Lambeau Field, coach Mike Holmgren called time-out and called over his star quarterback.

Holmgren proceeded to talk to Favre about the next play but paused as he saw Favre looking squarely at Holmgren's face, smiling.

"What the hell are you doing?" Holmgren screamed. "Are you listening to me?"

Favre smiled again and nodded.

"Oh, sure, Mike, but your mustache is frozen and it looks like half of it is gone."

Holmgren sent Favre back to the huddle and smiled to himself because he knew his quarterback, always supremely confident in the worst circumstances, had this one under control.

Of course, the Packers have had their share of not-ready-for-prime-time quarterbacks. David Whitehurst and Blair Kiel and John Hadl and Jerry Tagge and Randy Johnson leap to mind.

So does Scott Hunter.

In 1972 Dan Devine, the taciturn but sharp coach who had been a psychology major in college, used some of what he learned on his quarterback.

Hunter could generously be called a game manager for those Packers, who relied on a thunderous running game and a solid defense to win most of their games that season.

Hunter started all 14 games, completed 43 percent of his passes, and managed just six touchdown passes (along with nine interceptions). So no one was holding a spot for him in the Hall of Fame.

But for the most part, in a history where the fortunes on the field have run hot and cold, the Packers have often had the quarterback to get the job done.

In the fishbowl that is Green Bay and under the view of Packers fans everywhere, the quarterback is under the kind of scrutiny and pressure that would break many players. But not the best of the best, and this list of the Packers' best quarterbacks of all time features some of the most elite players to ever step into the position.

Really, it comes down to three players who belong in that pantheon: Bart Starr, Brett Favre, and Aaron Rodgers.

The argument for each is compelling.

With all that information and with all that history to consider, here are the quarterbacks worthy of leading this all-star team.

BART STARR

Bart Starr was the architect of five championships in Green Bay, including the first two Super Bowls, in both of which he was named Most Valuable Player.

His statistics were never eye-popping; indeed, they were often just average, even in an era that did not emphasize the pass. But he was the consummate game manager who called his own plays and, more important, knew what plays to call.

His direction downfield of his aging teammates against the Dallas Cowboys in the legendary "Ice Bowl" in 1967 was considered by many of his teammates, and opponents, as the greatest drive in NFL history.

In 16 seasons with the Packers, he completed barely 57 percent of his passes and threw for a paltry 24,000 yards with 152 touchdowns and 138 interceptions.

But in the postseason Starr flourished. He went 9-1 (winning nine in a row), completing 61 percent of his passes with 15 touchdowns and just three interceptions. There may have never been a game manager like Starr and, perhaps more important, given the way the NFL is today, there may never be again.

Imagine there was a time that Starr, disillusioned and angry, almost never got the opportunity to shine. He had been a 17th-round draft pick in 1956 (the NFL draft was an endless 30 rounds back then), and in two seasons under head coach Lisle Blackbourn and one under Ray McLean, Starr had sputtered badly. In those three seasons he threw just 13 touchdown

Bart Starr

passes compared with 25 interceptions and the Packers posted a dismal 8-27-1 record.

He wasn't sure what his future in pro football even looked like at that stage, and then he heard that the Packers had hired a well-regarded but untested offensive coordinator from the New York Giants as their new coach.

His name was Vince Lombardi, and Starr recalled seeing him in an exhibition game the previous season. The Packers were playing the Giants and Starr was amazed as he saw Lombardi screaming at the Giants defense for its poor play.

Starr couldn't believe what he was seeing.

Now this guy was the new Packers coach and Starr was intrigued and terrified. But once he met with Lombardi and realized what the new coach expected from him, he went home that night and told his wife, Cherry, that the Packers, at last, were going to start winning.

Lombardi designated Starr as his "coach on the field," but this wasn't just the same tired euphemism. Lombardi saw that Starr's strength was as the guy who kept his head when chaos was all around him, and Starr would prove that time and time again.

The results were there for all to see. Five championships, including those first two Super Bowls.

Rival players understood all too well how important Starr was to the Packers and how, if he had not been the quarterback, the Packers might not have been as successful as they were.

Hailed by teammates and rivals alike as a smart, cool quarterback, he was always prepared and exactly the leader Lombardi wanted and needed.

But time moves on, and the powerful Packers of the early to mid-1960s got older and slower and more banged up—and that included Starr. He battled back from all manner of injury in his later years, including a terrifying incident prior to the 1971 season when he nearly bled to death after experimental shoulder surgery went badly.

Finally, after 16 seasons under center, Starr retired prior to training camp in 1972, one of the most beloved Packers in history and one of the most respected among his NFL brethren.

Starr even stayed around that season, helping head coach Dan Devine tutor quarterbacks, before moving on to various careers that included car sales and TV color analysis.

He took over for Devine as head coach in 1975 and lasted nine mostly unremarkable seasons. He was inducted in the Pro Football Hall of Fame in 1977 and, until health issues overtook him in recent seasons, was always a fixture at Packers games. Bart Starr died on May 26, 2019, at the age of 85.

Brett Favre

Brett Favre rewrote the record book and redefined what a quarterback could be.

Fearless and reckless, sometimes at once, he played the game with a childlike abandon that he never lost, even in his later seasons when the injuries piled up. True, he left Green Bay under a cloud of anger and recrimination, but Packers fans could never stay mad at Favre for long. Not after what he did for the franchise.

Under the tutelage of coach Mike Holmgren, Favre developed into a three-time league MVP and threw for more than 61,000 yards, with 442 touchdowns and 286 interceptions. More incredibly, he started 275 straight games, a record that may never be broken.

Brett Favre calling signals deep in Bears territory, 2002
PAUL CUTLER VIA WIKIMEDIA COMMONS

He led the Packers to one Super Bowl title and should have won another, and his exploits on the field could include throwing a 75-yard touchdown one series and throwing an interception from his knees the next.

Mercurial and brilliant and foolish and spectacular, Favre put Green Bay back on the NFL map. He played quarterback as though his hair was on fire and fans around the NFL loved him for it. They still do.

Packers fans will never forget that September afternoon in 1992 when his legend was born.

It is a story that has taken on the kind of mythic sheen that the "Ice Bowl" has attained over the decades. And every Packers fan insists they were on hand at Lambeau Field when the new kid with the strange last name led the Packers back to a last-minute win over the Cincinnati Bengals.

His quarterbacks coach at the time, Steve Mariucci, watched in horror and bemusement and awe as Favre invented formations and misidentified plays yet still had the presence of mind to make something positive out of a potential disaster.

In fact, Mariucci has often said that first game was Favre's career in microcosm. He did so much wrong but he didn't care. His competitiveness and innate intelligence and sheer physical skill overcame all the things he didn't know.

He would become the face and the heart of a Packers team that would become the league's gold standard for seven years—an eternity in the NFL.

Fans from all over would come just to watch Favre with the hope of seeing something they hadn't seen before. And usually they did.

Favre led the Packers for 15 seasons, setting nearly every NFL passing record there was to set, including passing yards (61,655) and touchdowns (442), both of which have since been eclipsed.

And, oh yes, interceptions.

Brett Favre threw a lot of interceptions. More, in fact, than any quarterback in the history of the game. Over his career, Favre threw a staggering 336 interceptions—286 with the Packers alone. Across his 20 years in the NFL (19 of which he was a starter), he never threw fewer than 13 interceptions in a season, except in 2009, and in three seasons he led the league in that category.

It is the only blot on his stellar career, but it is also the price teams paid for his often brilliant play—because that brilliance wasn't possible without him taking risks no other quarterback would take.

He thought nothing of throwing into double and even triple coverage because he was so confident in his arm strength and ability to deliver the ball exactly where it needed to be. Sometimes he succeeded; other times he did not.

He never backed down and never changed how he played. But he was also human and time was catching up to him.

After the 2007 season, and again after the 2008 season, Favre hinted that it might be time to retire. His father's death in 2004 had shattered him, Mike Holmgren's departure still bothered him years later, and the Packers were spinning their wheels in terms of being competitive for an NFC title.

And he wasn't getting any younger. The injuries that he had shaken off as a younger quarterback were now hitting him harder.

So the thought of retirement naturally began creeping into his head. He knew a young, talented, and increasingly restless Aaron Rodgers waited on the sidelines, and now Favre had the memory of a gut-wrenching NFC championship loss to the New York Giants still gnawing at him.

On a frigid, unforgiving night at Lambeau Field, the Packers let an opportunity to return to another Super Bowl slip away when Favre threw a ghastly, unnecessary interception in overtime.

The Giants marched down the field and kicked the game-winning field goal and went to the Super Bowl.

Favre had thrown bad interceptions before and Packers fans had shrugged their shoulders and accepted it as part and parcel of the mercurial genius that had always been Brett Favre.

But this one was different. It was a bad throw at the worst time and, more perplexing, he didn't even seem like he cared that the turnover had cost his team a Super Bowl appearance.

The criticism was withering and nonstop. And the whispers now came out in full throat—Was Favre done? Were his best days behind him? Were the mistakes too egregious to ignore? Was it time to hand the job to Rodgers, the former first-round draft pick who had served his apprenticeship, and see what he could do?

It all piled up on Favre until finally, in a dramatic, tearful press conference that spring of 2008, Favre announced his retirement.

"It's not that I don't want to play," he said though his tears. "It's just I don't think I can anymore."

The announcement left the NFL, football fans around the world, and, especially, Packers fans stupefied. Could Brett Favre, who needed football like oxygen, really retire? It seemed unthinkable.

In fact, it was.

Almost as soon as Favre had made his announcement, reports came in a flurry that he was reconsidering. He was still raw from the playoff loss, he was still in physical as well as emotional pain, and he had taken the criticism too much to heart.

He had made a rash decision and now he wanted to take it back. Unfortunately for Favre and his legion of fans, the Packers took him at his word and they indeed moved on.

General manager Ted Thompson and head coach Mike McCarthy thanked Favre for his years of incomparable service, wished him the best, and handed the job of starting QB to Aaron Rodgers.

In a drama of Shakespearean proportions, Favre hunkered down in negotiations to win back his job while Rodgers doggedly went through training camp as the top guy.

Eventually, it became clear that too much damage had been done on both sides. The Packers had looked heartless in their dealings with the greatest quarterback the franchise had ever known. Meanwhile, Favre had looked opportunistic and selfish in his attempt to take back what he thought was rightfully his.

In the end, the Packers dealt Favre to the New York Jets for a fourth-round draft pick. Rodgers went on to throw for more than 4,000 yards, but the Packers stumbled to a 6-10 record.

Favre started all 16 games for the Jets, throwing for more than 3,400 yards with 22 touchdowns and 22 interceptions. After a promising start, the Jets lost four of their final five games and finished 9-7 and out of playoff contention.

Then Favre retired again. This time for good, he said.

That's when the Minnesota Vikings came calling and, in a move that enraged most Packers fans and damaged his relationship with Green Bay, he signed with the team's mortal rival.

Worse for Packers fans, many of whom still believed Favre should be under center in Green Bay, he played out of his mind his first season with the Vikings.

It was 2009 but he was playing like it was 10 years earlier. He threw for 4,202 yards, his best since 1998, and 33 touchdown passes, his best since 1997. He helped lead the Vikings to a 12-4 record, beating the Packers and Aaron Rodgers twice along the way, and helped send the Vikings to the NFC Championship Game.

But in overtime of that title game against the New Orleans Saints, bad-boy Brett Favre once again came out to play. Needing just 15 yards for a possible game-winning field goal to put the Vikings in the Super Bowl, Favre rolled right, threw back to the left across his body, and was intercepted. That set up the

Saints' game-winning field goal and they went to the Super Bowl.

Vikings fans howled in disbelief and Packers fans smiled and said, "That's our Brett."

That would be his last hurrah as the quarterback everyone knew. The Vikings begged him to return for one more season, convinced the pieces were still in place for another title run. They even sent a contingent of players down to his Mississippi compound to convince him.

Finally, he agreed. And it was a disaster.

He threw only 11 touchdown passes but 19 interceptions in 13 games, and the Vikings sputtered. Favre was actually knocked unconscious after he was tackled and his head hit the frozen turf in Minneapolis. Then, the next week, a December 28 game in Philadelphia, Favre's remarkable and unbreakable record-setting consecutive-games starting steak finally ended due to a shoulder injury. His replacement? A guy named Joe Webb, who has become an answer to a trivia question.

Favre was done. Finally. Completely.

And in the final act of the drama, Aaron Rodgers was named MVP as he led the Packers over the Pittsburgh Steelers to win the Super Bowl.

In the years that followed, Favre and the Packers organization agreed that both sides could have handled their divorce better. Now it was time for the two sides to reconcile. The only question was whether Packers fans would have anything to do with it.

The answer came on a hot July evening in 2015 when the Packers inducted Favre into their Hall of Fame and retired his number 4. On hand were 70,000 of his closest friends in a sold-out and raucous Lambeau Field. All was forgiven and all was forgotten.

The next year, he was inducted into the Pro Football Hall of Fame and he made it clear that while he finished his career in Minnesota, he was, and always would be, a Packer.

His records have stood the test of time and, in many cases, they will never be touched. He brought the Packers from obscurity to champions, and he did it all with a smile on his face.

AARON RODGERS

The entire football world watched as Aaron Rodgers stewed.

Embarrassed and shocked and burning with an anger he didn't even know he possessed, the University of California quarterback, projected by many as the top quarterback in the 2005 NFL draft, had yet to be selected as the first round wound to a close.

It's an old story now but still a good one, a story that speaks to perseverance and belief in self and, yes, good old-fashioned revenge.

Sitting in the 24th spot of that draft's first round were the Packers who, frankly, didn't need a quarterback because Brett Favre was still at the height of his wizardry.

But even general manager Ted Thompson, deliberate and calculating most times, could not pass up this quarterback. Because he knew one day Brett Favre would not be there and they needed someone special who would be.

For three years Rodgers watched and waited for his opportunity and picked up what he could from the incumbent Favre, who often said, both publicly and privately, that it was not his job to train his understudy.

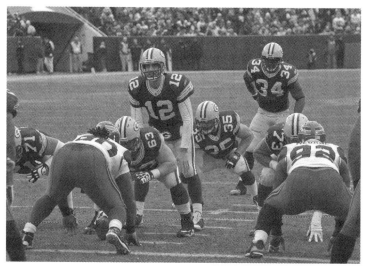

Aaron Rodgers
MIKE MORBECK VIA WIKIMEDIA COMMONS

So Rodgers observed and learned, mostly on his own, devouring all the information he could about reading rival defenses, learning the Packers offense, and watching Favre, who showed the young quarterback, whether he had planned to or not, how to play the position through good times and bad.

In a November 29, 2007, game against the Dallas Cowboys, Rodgers showed the first intriguing signs of the quarterback he would one day become.

Favre was already playing poorly, having thrown two first-half interceptions, but then he was injured in the third quarter and in stepped Rodgers.

Looking poised and more confident than anyone might have expected, he went on to complete 19 of 26 passes for 201 yards and his first TD pass (to Greg Jennings), and nearly led the Packers back to victory.

Rodgers made his debut as the Packers' starting quarterback on a Monday night against the Minnesota Vikings. It was September 8, 2008, and it was the first time in 16 years that anyone other than Favre started a game as Green Bay's quarterback. He completed 18 of 22 passes for 178 yards, throwing for one score and running for another. The Aaron Rodgers era had begun, though few knew it yet.

All he has done since is prove to be perhaps the best quarterback in the NFL. His combination of arm strength, mobility, confidence, and intelligence has put him among the game's all-time greats.

A two-time league MVP, he led the Packers to a Super Bowl title in 2010. Indeed, it was his performance in that strange 2010 season that put Rodgers among the game's best.

It was a season that saw the Packers battle injuries and inconsistency, including losing Rodgers for a game and a half due to a concussion. The Packers lost both games and found themselves at 8-6 and facing the task of winning their final two games just to qualify for the playoffs.

Rodgers returned in the first must-win game against the New York Giants and threw for 404 yards and four touchdowns in a decisive victory. Then he helped the Packers battle past the Chicago Bears to gain a postseason berth.

Little was expected from Green Bay in the postseason as the sixth, and lowest, seed, but Rodgers found a new level that would eventually result in the Packers' fourth Super Bowl title and him being named the game's MVP.

In the three playoff games, all played on the road, the Packers beat the Philadelphia Eagles, Atlanta Falcons, and Chicago Bears. In that span he completed 90 of 132 passes for nine touchdowns and just two interceptions. He also ran for one touchdown.

He was especially impressive against the highly favored Falcons as he completed 31 of 36 passes for 366 yards and three scores in a 48–21 win.

In the Super Bowl win over the Steelers, Rodgers completed 24 of 39 passes for 404 yards and three touchdowns and was named the game's MVP.

Since then, he has found himself on a level to which every quarterback aspires but most never even get close.

But there have also been no Super Bowl appearances since then, and if there's a knock on Rodgers, that's it.

Through the 2018 season, he has completed 64.8 percent of his passes and his interception percentage is a stunning 1.5. By comparison, Favre's was 3.3. Rodgers makes throws few other quarterbacks even attempt and he does what a quarterback is supposed to do: make everyone around him better.

Evidence of that was obvious in 2017 when the Packers, with a healthy Rodgers, were 4-1. When he was lost for much of the season with a broken collarbone, the Packers slid to 3-6 and missed the playoffs. He is the face of the Packers and that is no small assignment.

AND THE WINNER IS . . .

Now this is a tough call. In fact, if this were an election, the final result might hinge on absentee ballots and then it all could still lead to a recount.

Bart Starr was the epitome of the kind of quarterback every coach, no matter the generation, would love to have. Never possessed of great physical skills, he was smart and unflappable and those skills are rare indeed. Recall what his teammates said in the huddle of that final drive of the "Ice Bowl."

While all around him was chaos, Starr was preternaturally calm, convinced his teammates had what it took for one last dramatic statement.

"When we saw Bart's eyes, we knew we were going to win," said guard Jerry Kramer. And they did. He was indeed a winner, a two-time Super Bowl MVP and the perfect quarterback to run Lombardi's offense. He occupies few spots in the team record book when it comes to all-time passing leaders except this—two-time Super Bowl champ. His number 15 was retired by the Packers, and in 1977 he was inducted into the Pro Football Hall of Fame.

You never knew what you'd get with Brett Favre. He was a ball of kinetic energy who could be counted on to make either the most incredible play that led to victory or, just as likely, a bizarre lapse that would seal a defeat. He could throw four touchdowns in one game and four interceptions the next, but he made every decision at full speed and, usually, without regret. After all, his mantra was make a play or don't bother playing at all. It was an attitude that made him the most entertaining quarterback of his era but also kept him from reaching even greater heights. Lots of great, memorable plays coupled with just as many unforced mistakes made him the quarterback you couldn't look away from but couldn't necessarily trust either.

Aaron Rodgers is the rolling glacier compared to Brett Favre's all-compassing forest fire. Possessing Starr's calm and controlled demeanor, Favre's strong arm (OK, maybe not quite as strong), and a technical perfection that neither of the other two possessed, Rodgers has been one of the game's great quarterbacks for a decade.

Some believe he's been held back by the relatively conservative coaching of Mike McCarthy and a cast of less-than-superb offensive talent. With a different system, just maybe, he could set passing records no one would approach.

During a disastrous 2018 season when the Packers went 6-9-1, Rodgers injured his knee in the season opener but played through it all season. Clearly, though, his relationship with McCarthy had soured, and after a late-season loss to the pathetic Arizona Cardinals, McCarthy was fired. Many observers believe Rodgers was the reason for McCarthy's dismissal and Rodgers absorbed his share of criticism for that perception. It was not a great season for Rodgers, but consider this: He still threw for 4,442 yards and 25 touchdowns (and he missed most of the season finale with a concussion). He also threw just two interceptions, setting an NFL record along the way with 402 pass attempts without an interception.

With a new coach in Matt LaFleur and a new attitude, Rodgers should reclaim his spot as the game's best. And his reservation in Canton is assured, though another Super Bowl title or two wouldn't hurt his reputation.

So here's what it comes down to on our all-star team. Great players at every position need a great quarterback, and any one of these three finalists could handle the job superbly.

It's hard to say what matters most—the cool efficiency of Bart Starr, the football genius of Brett Favre, or the frightening exactitude of Aaron Rodgers.

So let's go with this: Our all-stars need a 90-yard drive to win the game, and there's one minute and 53 seconds left to play in a cold rainstorm in Chicago. Who's the choice?

With a game on the line when the skill required is something close to perfection, it has to be **Aaron Rodgers**.

QUARTERBACKS WHO DID NOT MAKE THE CUT

For a few years in the late 1970s and early '80s, **Lynn Dickey** triggered one of the most entertaining offenses in the NFL. Many NFL observers at the time considered Dickey the best deep-ball thrower in the league. In nine seasons (he missed an entire season with a badly broken leg), he threw for more than 21,000 yards and 133 touchdowns. His 4,458 passing yards in 1983 was a team record until it was broken by Rodgers's 4,643 in 2011. But as good as the offense was in those years, the defense for the most part was horrendous. And that's why Dickey had only one playoff appearance.

Arnie Herber was a Green Bay native who played 11 seasons for the Packers (1930–40) and was considered one of the first great long passers in league history thanks to his deadly combination with Don Hutson. He threw for more than 8,000 yards and 81 touchdowns and led the Packers to four NFL titles. He was inducted into the Pro Football Hall of Fame in 1966.

FULLBACK

The Candidates

Jim Taylor
William Henderson
Clarke Hinkle

In today's NFL, this iconic position has mostly gone the way of the leather helmet. Most NFL teams no longer even keep a fullback on the roster, content to add another wide receiver, an offensive lineman, or a fullback hybrid called an H back or something else.

To their credit, the Packers had kept the position on their roster for years after most other teams had moved on. But even the Packers had to make concessions to the current state of the NFL and in 2018, for the first time in years, there was no fullback on the roster. That could change, of course, because the NFL is nothing if not transient.

But for now, the fullback has gone the way of eight-track tapes and fax machines.

So let's take a stroll through history at a position that has meant so much to the Packers over the years.

JIM TAYLOR

In the old NFL, the position of fullback had a certain swagger. It was played by tough, strong, and mean guys who could not only run and catch passes but also block. They had the mentality of running through a defender instead of around him, and when asked why, they would reply, "Why not?"

The fullback was the featured position in the NFL of the 1950s and '60s, and no one epitomized that rugged role better than the Packers' Jim Taylor.

Indeed, Philadelphia Eagles star quarterback Norm Van Brocklin once said of Taylor, as reported on Packers.com, "He's tougher than Japanese arithmetic."

He looked every bit like a fullback, with his twisted nose that had broken more times than he could count, his trademark crew cut, and a look that told defenders to tackle him at their own risk. He looked menacing and he ran in just the same fashion.

In the 1960s, Taylor, along with halfback Paul Hornung, formed a withering backfield combination that left rival defenses uncertain of just what to do. And when Taylor or Hornung swept the corner running the celebrated and destructive

Jim Taylor's 1961 Topps card
TOPPS COMPANY VIA WIKIMEDIA COMMONS

"Packers Sweep," many defenders simply braced for what was to come.

Unfortunately for Taylor, he probably didn't get all the accolades he deserved since he played at the same time as Jim Brown, the Cleveland Browns' incomparable fullback who is still considered perhaps the greatest running back of all time and certainly the first dominant running back in NFL history.

But Packers coach Vince Lombardi always said this about the two men: "Jim Brown would give a defender his leg and take it away from him. Jim Taylor would give a defender his leg and ram it through his chest."

He remains the Packers' second-leading rusher all-time with 8,207 yards, and his 81 rushing touchdowns (of 91 total TDs) are still a team record that may never be broken. His single-game rushing record of 186 yards against the New York Giants in 1961 lasted for 36 years and, despite 2,166 touches, he fumbled just 34 times.

And his last season with the Packers was in 1966.

It was a different time in America and certainly in the NFL, and there were no guarantees that a player like Taylor, despite a stellar college career at LSU, would even get a shot.

So when Packers personnel and scouting director Jerry Vainisi received a letter from Taylor all but begging for an opportunity to prove he could play fullback in the NFL, Vainisi took it to heart and made him the Packers' second-round draft pick in 1958. It was the same draft that produced Hall of Fame linebacker Ray Nitschke and guard Jerry Kramer as well as another prominent starter in linebacker Dan Currie.

Still, Taylor must have wondered what he had stepped into that first season as the Packers staggered to a 1-10-1 record, the worst mark in team history.

Worse for him, he barely got off the bench the first 10 weeks of the season—apparently, according to head coach Ray McLean, because he didn't know the offense.

He actually had to play behind second-year back Paul Hornung, who was already growing frustrated in his own right because he felt McLean wasn't using him properly.

Taylor finally got his chance in the final two games of that lost season and responded by gaining 137 yards against the San Francisco 49ers and another 99 yards against the Los Angeles Rams. His 247 rushing yards constituted the third-best on the team that season.

But everything changed the following season when Vince Lombardi took over as head coach. Committed to running the football, Lombardi looked to Taylor and halfback Paul Hornung to be his workhorses and they gladly obliged.

That first season, Taylor rushed for 452 yards and six touchdowns as the Packers rebounded with a 7-5 record. What followed were five straight seasons of more than 1,000 yards rushing, including a league-high 1,474 yards in 1962 when the Packers went 13-1. The season was capped with Green Bay's second straight NFL title as they went to New York and, in miserably cold and windy conditions on a Yankee Stadium field with the consistency of a parking lot, beat the Giants, 16–7.

Taylor has always called this his finest game, as he rushed for 85 yards on 31 carries and scored one touchdown despite a gash on his elbow that required seven stitches to close and a lacerated tongue—both compliments of Giants linebacker Sam Huff.

After the game even the rugged Huff offered grudging respect.

"Taylor isn't human," he said. "No human being could have taken the punishment he got today."

Taylor was the leading rusher in four of Green Bay's five championship seasons and scored the first Packers touchdown in the inaugural Super Bowl against the Kansas City Chiefs.

In 1967, after playing out his option (brought on more than a little by a contract dispute with Lombardi), Taylor signed with the expansion New Orleans Saints.

Taylor didn't have much of a season with the struggling Saints, rushing for 390 yards and catching 38 passes. After that he retired and remained with the Saints as a radio color commentator and then as a traveling scout.

Taylor was inducted into the Pro Football Hall of Fame in 1976 and was named to the NFL All-Decade Team of the 1960s. He was also named to the Packers' 50th Anniversary Team, their All-Modern Era Team, and the All-Century squad, and was inducted into the Packers Hall of Fame in 1975.

The rugged Taylor, perhaps the eternal image of a Green Bay Packers football player, died in October 2018 at age 83.

WILLIAM HENDERSON

Look for any statistic that separates William Henderson from other fullbacks who have lined up for the Packers, and it will be hard to find.

Except for this: game after game and year after year, William Henderson was there, unceremoniously and unselfishly doing the job that needed to be done.

He was a third-round draft pick in 1995, the same draft that produced four other starters (cornerback Craig Newsome, linebacker Brian Williams, wide receiver Antonio Freeman, and guard Adam Timmerman) and the draft that very likely provided the final bricks for the foundation of a team that would dominate the NFL for five years.

William Henderson (33) pregame, 2003
WIKIMEDIA COMMONS

And in 12 seasons, Henderson, playing a position in which violent collisions came on just about every play, missed exactly four games. His 188 games played is fifth all-time in franchise history.

Henderson was a fullback in every sense of the word. He was under no illusions about his running ability since in his 12 seasons, he carried the ball just 123 times for 426 yards. His best rushing season was 1996, when he carried 39 times for 130 yards. In fact, as the Packers offense evolved over the years, Henderson carried the ball exactly one time in his final five seasons.

But the guy could block. And he could catch passes.

Variously nicknamed "Boogie" and "Big Stiffy" by quarterback Brett Favre, Henderson had the size and power to open as a lead blocker for 1,000-yard rushers like Edgar Bennett, Dorsey Levens, and Ahman Green.

"I always knew my role," he said.

But where he was also a force on offense was coming out of the backfield and catching passes. Blessed with remarkably soft hands for a guy who stood 6-foot-1 and weighed 250 pounds, he was a load for defenders to tackle after he grabbed a pass and headed upfield.

He finished his career with 320 receptions for 2,409 yards and 14 touchdowns. His best season was 1997, when he caught 41 passes, but between 1996 and 2005 he never caught fewer than 21 passes. Through 2018, he is still 15th on the Packers' all-time receptions list and only Ahman Green has caught more as a running back.

Henderson was a reliable piece of a powerful puzzle that, in his 12 seasons, saw the Packers go to two Super Bowls and experience just one losing season.

After the 2006 season, Henderson sensed the Packers had other plans for the fullback position. And he was right. But, showing the kind of respect to a veteran who had given so much to the Packers, they released him in early spring so he'd have an opportunity to catch on with another team.

But after so many years in one place, Henderson had no desire to play anywhere else.

"Everyone talks about how green the grass is on the other side, but I didn't see it that way," Henderson told Fox News. "Green Bay is a small market, yes. You can't get a great meal after 10 o'clock at night. It's not Dallas or Atlanta or New York, so it is limiting. But you knew what you were there for.

"I became a man in Green Bay and Wisconsin had become home for me. It is a very special feeling knowing that every career special moment I had happened with the Packers. I was spiritually blessed to land in Green Bay, of all places. Running through those tunnels like the Packers' founding fathers had who did it with style and with class, I got to follow in their footsteps. I got a chance to play for the best organization in sports, the best franchise there is."

Henderson was named to the 2004 Pro Bowl and, more important to him, he was inducted into the Packers Hall of Fame in 2011.

CLARKE HINKLE

The early years of the National Football League, when players wore leather helmets and chips on their shoulders, was known as the "Iron Man Era."

The game was played by tough, driven, sometimes fanatical men for whom the toughest yards were the only yards worth gaining.

Specialists? There were no such things. The guys who played in the 1920s, '30s, and '40s played wherever they were needed because—well, that was what was required. So a running back would play linebacker and a defensive back would play wide receiver.

And back in the days when the NFL was something more like a controlled street fight, Clarke Hinkle stood tall.

He was a fullback and a halfback. He could play quarterback and he was a great linebacker. And he was also the Packers' field goal kicker and the game's best punter. Some NFL observers of the time called him "the greatest football player in the world today."

Enough?

Curly Lambeau saw Hinkle playing in a college all-star game in January 1932 and signed him to play for the Packers, who by that point had become the finest team in the NFL. Lambeau made Hinkle his starting fullback, and a Hall of Fame career was off and running.

"I wanted to play so bad that I would have signed for nothing," Hinkle once said, as reported on Packers.com.

Teammates and opponents alike considered him the most dedicated and driven player they'd ever seen. Chicago Bears Hall of Fame linebacker Clyde "Bulldog" Turner told Cliff Christl of Packers.com, "He was the hardest runner I ever tried to tackle. When you hit him, it would just pop every joint all the way down to your toes."

Teammate Bob Adkins was more succinct: "He was meaner than a rattlesnake."

Another teammate, quarterback Cecil Isbell, remembered just how important every game was to Hinkle.

"Before every game, he'd get glassy-eyed, he'd be so fired up and eager to play," Isbell said in a Packers.com story. "After the game, if we lost, he'd sit at his locker and cry like a baby."

Hinkle was perhaps the first great Packers running back, rushing for 3,860 yards from 1932 to 1941. That's still seventh-best in team history, and his 1,171 carries remains the fourth most all-time seven decades later.

But as good as he was on offense (he also caught 49 passes, kicked 28 field goals, and averaged 40.8 yards on punts), many believed he was even better on defense.

From his linebacker spot, Hinkle was a ferocious tackler and his battles with Chicago Bears running back Bronko Nagurski, a fellow Hall of Famer, were legendary.

"My goal was to get to the Bronk before he got to me," Hinkle said. One memorable collision occurred in 1934 when the two men met on a sideline tackle and Nagurski, two inches taller and 30 pounds heavier, had to leave the game with a fractured rib and broken nose.

But the two respected each other and became good friends, and in 1964, when Hinkle was inducted into the Pro Football Hall of Fame, he asked Nagurski to introduce him.

On the podium, Nagurski cracked, "They said I was tough to tackle, but this guy here didn't have too much trouble."

Hinkle was an All-Pro every year he played and was named to the NFL All-Decade Team for the 1930s, the Packers' 50th Anniversary Team, and the Packers' All-Iron Man Era Team.

He enlisted in the Coast Guard in 1942 when World War II broke out and did not return to football but stayed with the Packers as a scout. He remained close to the organization the rest of his life (he died in 1988 at the age of 79), and in 1997 the Packers named their main practice field on Oneida Street after Hinkle.

AND THE WINNER IS . . .

This is a battle between two serious heavyweights—Jim Taylor and Clarke Hinkle. They were from different eras but they played the game the same way—by leaving everything on the field. And both are Hall of Famers who all these years later remain inextricably tied to the Packers and their legacy.

Five decades after he played, Taylor remains one of the great running backs in the NFL and an icon of the Green Bay Packers. He played in an era when the NFL running back was becoming something truly special. He joined Cleveland's Jim Brown as the two runners who combined power and speed and determination to redefine the fullback position. And, ironically, Taylor often outplayed Brown when the two teams met.

Clarke Hinkle was the kind of player that the NFL was built upon, a two-way monster who could tackle and run and play with the kind of abandon that made him both feared and respected.

Taylor only played fullback for the Packers, but he redefined the position and helped make the Packers a dynasty in the 1960s. Hinkle was good at any position, so it's hard to know where to put him.

As for William Henderson, he was a fine fullback who played with an intensity and a desire that both Taylor and Hinkle would have admired.

So in a close, testy, physical vote—exactly as it should be when choosing an all-star Packers fullback—this is at its essence a truly fullback position, and in the long, storied history of the Packers, the name that continues to resonate is **Jim Taylor**.

FULLBACKS WHO DID NOT MAKE THE CUT

John Kuhn was a true fan favorite, a long shot who came to the Packers as a free agent in 2007, after a college career at Shippensburg State and one season with the Pittsburgh Steelers. He hung with the Packers for nine seasons primarily as a blocking back, and when he did carry the ball, the fans went crazy, yelling "KOOOOOOON" in response. In his nine seasons, he rushed for 601 yards and 15 touchdowns and caught 81 passes for another eight scores. He was also a two-time Pro Bowler. He left Green Bay in 2016 to play for the New Orleans Saints, but fans still miss him and his dedication to giving his all on every play. He played two seasons for the Saints but missed the 2018 season due to injury. After the season, Kuhn returned to Green Bay to announce his retirement as a Packer. "He was a true professional whose work ethic and leadership set a great example both on the field and in the locker room," said Packers general manager Brian Gutekunst.

MacArthur Lane only spent three seasons with the Packers (1972–74) after he was traded by the St. Louis Cardinals. But they were productive seasons for him and relatively successful seasons for the Packers. In 1972 he teamed with halfback John Brockington to form the NFL's most dynamic backfield. While he blocked for Brockington, who ran for more than 1,000 yards, Lane also rushed for 821 yards of his own and caught 26 passes. That tandem helped Green Bay reach the playoffs for the first time in five years. In his three seasons in Green Bay, he rushed for 1,711 yards and caught 87 passes. He went on to play four more seasons with the Kansas City Chiefs.

Lost in the shuffle of big men who played even bigger is **Gerry Ellis**, who was a sometime fullback and a part-time halfback. Not small by any means, 5-foot-11 and 220 pounds, he was from a different mold. He is 20th in team history in receptions with 267 and eighth all-time in rushing with 3,826 yards. So he could do it all. He was unfortunately stuck on Packers teams from 1980 to 1986 that were thunderously mediocre, so he never got the national exposure he probably deserved. Still, he was inducted into the Packers Hall of Fame in 1994.

HALFBACK

The Candidates
Paul Hornung
Ahman Green
Tony Canadeo

In the old days the position was known as a halfback. In today's NFL it's tailback. But, really, the goal is the same. Yes, the NFL has tilted dramatically toward throwing the ball, but if teams can't run, especially with a game on the line or in bad weather, success rarely follows. The Packers have known a parade of wonderful ruinning backs going back to the days of Curly Lambeau and continuing even until today.

In truth, the Packers have not had a truly game-changing back since Ahman Green, but they don't come around often anway. But the search is always on to find that back who can make a difference. And, often, he can be found in places no one is really looking.

PAUL HORNUNG
For as long as he could remember, he was known as "the Golden Boy." And Paul Hornung did nothing to dissuade the talk.

Paul Hornung and Vince Lombardi in the 1960s
AP IMAGES/NFL PHOTOS

He was a star in every stop he made. He was a spectacular high school athlete—excelling in football, baseball, and basketball—in his hometown of Louisville, Kentucky.

He took his football talents to the University of Notre Dame, where he again flourished, winning the Heisman Trophy in 1956 as he played running back and quarterback as well as defensive back.

So when he was taken with the first pick of the 1957 NFL draft by the moribund Green Bay Packers, it was expected he would step in and change the team's fortunes—because that's what players like him did.

Hornung eventually did just that, helping the Packers to dominate the NFL from his halfback position. And he did it his way.

Funny and handsome and rakish, he lived life his way and flaunted authority and convention whenever he could.

He mingled with Hollywood starlets and Las Vegas entertainers. He pushed the envelope every chance he could and it would finally cost him in 1963, when he was suspended for a season for his dealings with gamblers—a charge he never denied.

He exasperated his head coach, Vince Lombardi, on dozens of occasions, but Hornung remained one of Lombardi's all-time favorite players and was handpicked to be one of Lombardi's pallbearers at his funeral in 1970.

Paul Hornung was a very good NFL player who could have been so much better if he had avoided injuries and, perhaps, paid more attention to the game he liked but never loved. Indeed, when he finally earned his spot in the Pro Football Hall of Fame in 1986, no one was more surprised because he was convinced his past exploits had cost him entry into that exclusive club.

But through it all, Hornung never backed away from who he was or what he did or how he did it.

For that larger-than-life image, and because when he was healthy he was an incomparable back, he has earned his place as a candidate for a spot on this roster.

But for the first few seasons of his Packers career, it seemed he'd flame out through a combination of poor coaching and a bad attitude.

Hornung came to a Packers team in the throes of nine straight nonwinning seasons. His first coach, Lisle Blackbourn, knew Hornung had played both quarterback and halfback at Notre Dame but he didn't think he threw well enough to be an NFL quarterback.

So Blackbourn moved him to the backfield, where he rushed for just 319 yards his first season. When Ray McLean stepped in as head coach the next season, his view of Hornung did not change. Stuck at halfback, he managed just 310 rushing yards.

Frustrated and already sick of losing after just two seasons, Hornung gave serious consideration to quitting and pursuing a career as an actor.

But in 1959 the Packers hired Vince Lombardi as head coach and, just a few weeks after the announcement, he sent a handwritten letter to Hornung, advising him to come to training in great shape because he was going to use him in ways he never imagined.

Intrigued, Hornung did indeed come to camp in the best shape of his life, and Lombardi was better than his word. He saw in Hornung a multifaceted offensive threat who could run, throw, catch passes, and kick—and Lombardi planned to use him in every way he could.

From 1959 to 1961 he was the NFL's leading scorer. In 1960 alone Hornung scored 176 points (13 rushing and 2 receiving touchdowns, 15 field goals, and 41 extra points), an NFL record that stood until 2006 when San Diego running back LaDainian Tomlinson scored 186 points.

In his career, Hornung rushed for 3,711 yards and scored 760 points, which remains fifth all-time in team history. And this despite missing the entire 1963 season due to his suspension.

When he returned in 1964, though, injuries plagued him and he missed the Packers' victory in the first Super Bowl. Prior to the 1967 season, he was selected by the New Orleans Saints in the expansion draft, a move that devastated Lombardi.

But Hornung was suffering from a serious neck injury and was told in no uncertain terms by doctors that if he continued to play, he'd eventually be paralyzed. So Hornung retired.

He returned to Green Bay and was on the sidelines with Lombardi during the "Ice Bowl," standing so close to the coach that he asked Hornung for advice on play calls.

Hornung did some TV color commentary work, acted a little, and ran successful companies, but mostly he has enjoyed being a former Green Bay Packer.

He still lives in Louisville and, while retired from his business ventures, he continues to keep his eye on everything he has been involved in. He remains devoted to the Packers, having been inducted into the team's Hall of Fame in 1975.

For Hornung, though, the cap to his career was finally earning a spot in the Pro Football Hall of Fame. His season-long suspension in 1963 for his association with gamblers was one he accepted from NFL commissioner Pete Rozelle even though he insisted he did nothing worse than many other players of the era.

And he knew that suspension would cost him in the eyes of those with Hall of Fame induction votes—especially sportswriters with whom he had always had a fractious relationship.

Finally, however, Hornung's versatility and, frankly, his acceptance of his penalty made a difference with enough voters that he was elected in 1986.

"Greatest honor of my life," he said.

Even today he revels in his former career and, mostly, in his celebrity. He knows as well as anyone that his career could have been even better than it was if not for injuries and bad decisions. But he has no regrets.

Ahman Green

Was the deal that sent cornerback Fred Vinson to the Seattle Seahawks for a fumble-prone running back named Ahman Green the greatest trade in Packers history?

Well, of course not. After all, the deal that brought a quarterback named Brett Favre to Green Bay from Atlanta for a first-round draft pick might rank up there, too.

Nonetheless, when Ahman Green was dealt to the Packers in 2000 for Vinson and a fifth-round draft pick, few gave it much thought.

Green, who knew the Midwest after growing up in Omaha, Nebraska, and who starred at the University of Nebraska, still wasn't sure Green Bay would be the place for him. But he admitted years later that the trade was a blessing in disguise and that, indeed, playing for the Packers was the ideal placement for him.

Ahman Green moves the ball against the Seahawks.
MIKE MORBECK VIA WIKIMEDIA COMMONS

The Packers also learned that Green was the perfect addition for a team looking to the next era after back-to-back Super Bowl appearances in 1996 and 1997. Dorsey Levens, who had been the key workhorse tailback in the Mike Holmgren years, was aging and losing effectiveness. And Holmgren had moved on, replaced by Mike Sherman.

Green stepped right in as Green Bay's starting tailback in 2000 and rushed for 1,175 yards (which took its place as 10th best in team history) and caught 73 passes.

He had only three games where he rushed for more than 100 yards, and all came in the final six weeks of the season. His first 100-yard rushing effort came when he gashed the Indianapolis Colts for 153 yards on 24 carries. His best performance came three weeks later when he ran 25 times for 161 yards against the Vikings.

If there was any doubt earlier that Green was the answer at running back for the Packers, his late-season surge ended it.

He would go on to rush for more than 1,000 yards in the following four seasons as well, including a team record 1,883 yards in 2003. In fact, of the Packers' top 10 single-season rushing performances, Green still owns four of them through the 2018 season.

But the years are especially tough on NFL running backs, and injuries, mostly of the nagging kind, piled up and caught up with Green. And, as was the case six years earlier, the Packers were looking to the next generation of running back and the younger, stronger Ryan Grant took Green's role.

A free agent heading into the 2007 season, Green signed with the Houston Texans and his old Packers coach, Mike Sherman, who was now offensive coordinator with the Texans. But injuries continued to plague him and he played only 14 games in two seasons before the Texans released him.

Green returned to the Packers in 2009 in a limited role, and in a November 8 game against the Tampa Bay Buccaneers, he rushed for 45 yards on six carries and moved past the iconic Jim Taylor as the Packers' all-time leading rusher.

Green's Packers career ended at the conclusion of that season, and his 8,322 yards remains the team's all-time rushing record. Taylor, who had held the mark for 43 years, rushed for 8,207 yards.

Upon having his mark broken, Taylor said he could not have been happier for Green.

And for Green, who was traded to the Packers almost as an afterthought, the record means everything. He knows his name sits above the likes of Packers legends like Paul Hornung, Tony Canadeo, and Clarke Hinkle—who are all in the Pro Football Hall of Fame.

Green also holds the record for career rushing yards at Lambeau Field (4,507), most rushing yards in a game at Lambeau (218 vs. the Denver Broncos in 2003), and longest run from scrimmage at Lambeau (98 yards vs. Denver in 2003).

Green did try to keep his pro career going, first in the now-defunct United Football League and then in a tryout with Montreal in the Canadian Football League. But injuries persisted and he retired.

Green, who was inducted into the Packers Hall of Fame in 2014, has remained in the Green Bay area in the intervening years, running several organizations, including an Alzheimer's disease awareness foundation and a Green Bay indoor football league team, of which he is part owner.

TONY CANADEO

One of the most beloved Packers in history, Tony Canadeo's influence on the team lasted well beyond his playing days. And still persists.

He earned one of the great nicknames in sports while in college at Gonzaga University in Spokane, Washington. Prematurely gray-haired, he was called "the Gray Ghost of Gonzaga," and once with the Packers, it was shortened to simply "the Gray Ghost."

And in 11 seasons with the Packers, he would go from relatively unknown to one of only six players to have his number retired by the team.

Canadeo was a ninth-round pick in the 1941 draft and, like so many players in so many eras, he started at one position (quarterback) before being shifted to spots where he could excel.

Three stars were nearing the end of their careers—Cecil Isbell, Arnie Herber, and Clarke Hinkle—and Canadeo found himself in the right place at the right time.

Not particularly big or fast, even for the NFL of the 1940s, he displayed the kind of tenacity that overcame everything else. So he would become a star running back, kick returner, defensive back, and punter.

He would go on to become the Packers' first 1,000-yard rusher, and his 4,197 career rushing yards, amazingly, remains fourth all-time in team history—and his last season was in 1955. He also caught 69 passes, intercepted nine passes from his defensive back position, and was one of the era's top kickoff and punt returners.

Due to military service, Canadeo missed most of the 1944 season, which was the year the Packers beat the New York

Giants for their last NFL championship until 1961. World War II also forced him to miss the entire 1945 season, which marked the beginning of the Packers' nearly two-decade slide.

When Canadeo returned for the 1946 season, he found himself, and other NFL stars, being wooed by the rival All-America Football Conference, a precursor to the American Football League.

Canadeo turned down the new league and returned to the Packers, where he continued as a solid player, even as the Packers slowly began to slip on the field.

Coach Curly Lambeau, who had taken a chance on Canadeo and to whom Canadeo had remained loyal, was openly feuding with the Packers board of directors, and by 1949 it became clear that the team founder had to move on after 30 years.

Lambeau's final season, 1949, was Canadeo's first exclusively as a halfback and he waged a battle all season with the Philadelphia Eagles' Steve Van Buren for the NFL rushing title. The two were neck and neck until Van Buren pulled away in the final three games. Canadeo rushed for 1,052 yards while Van Buren won the title with 1,146.

The following season, under new coach Gene Ronzani, Canadeo was relegated to more of a blocking back for leading rusher Billy Grimes. Even in that role, he excelled.

"Tony Canadeo is one of the toughest players I ever played with," Grimes said afterward. "He did a lot of the blocking for me and that helped me a lot."

But by that stage, the Packers' spiral was in full motion. A 2-10 season in 1949 was followed by back-to-back 3-9 seasons, and after the 1952 season Canadeo retired.

He was a two-time All-Pro, a member of the NFL's 1940s All-Decade Team, and in 1974 was inducted into both the Pro

Football Hall of Fame and the Packers Hall of Fame. And in 1952 his number 3 was retired by the Packers, just the second number at that time (next to Don Hutson's 14) to receive the honor.

"My dream came true," he said simply.

Canadeo remained a fixture around Green Bay and the Packers for decades to follow. He did radio color analysis in the 1960s along with Ray Scott, was a member of the team's executive committee, and owned a metal manufacturing company in Green Bay.

He was a fixture at Packers games for years, and his death in 2003 at age 84 was mourned by Packers fans everywhere.

AND THE WINNER IS . . .

We'd all like to nod toward nostalgia and the man who still makes being a Green Bay Packer his cottage industry. But Paul Hornung is not the best running back in team history, and anyone who cares to argue the point is welcome to make the case.

Hornung was indeed a fine player who was badly utilized his first two seasons before Vince Lombardi figured out how to use him properly. Horning was versatile and talented and a major part of the juggernaut that was the Green Bay Packers of the 1960s.

Tony Canadeo, as well, exemplified the "Iron Man" age of the NFL by playing several different positions and excelling at all of them. He was the face of the Packers, and when his number 3 was just the second number retired in team history, it showed the esteem in which he was held.

But in the end, it's the numbers that matter and this number—8,322—is what matters most. He is the Green Bay Packers' all-time leading rusher and, quite possibly in this era when

NFL backs absorb the kind of physical abuse that leads to short careers, his record may never be broken. So, in another close vote, the choice here is **Ahman Green**.

HALFBACKS WHO DID NOT MAKE THE CUT

Johnny "Blood" McNally was a fiery free spirit who was so good at so many positions that it was difficult to place him in one spot. He played halfback from 1929 to 1936 for the Packers but he was also an excellent defensive back, punter, and receiver. He is perhaps most famous for his nickname, picked up after watching a movie called *Blood and Sand*. Also nicknamed "the Vagabond Halfback" for his penchant to switch teams, he played 14 NFL seasons for five teams—including seven seasons with the Packers. He could run, throw, and kick and many believed he was the finest receiver of the time. A member of the NFL's 1930s All-Decade Team, he was inducted into the Pro Football Hall of Fame in 1963 and the Packers Hall of Fame in 1970.

The selection of running back **Dorsey Levens** in the fifth round of the 1994 draft left little or no impression on many who watched the NFL. He was, after all, an oft-injured back in college, first at Notre Dame and then at Georgia Tech. But general manager Ron Wolf, as he so often did, saw something intriguing in Levens, who had the size (6-foot-1, 230 pounds) and the skills to make this increasingly powerful Packers team even better. And he did. In eight seasons with the Packers, he was a key member of both Super Bowl teams. In his career, which was punctuated by injury, he rushed for 3,937 yards, sixth-best in team history, and his 1,006 carries is fifth-best. He also caught 271 passes, which still ranks in the top 20 in team history. After leaving the Packers, Levens played two seasons for the Eagles and one for the Giants. He now works on studying the effects of concussions on NFL players and occasionally acts. He was inducted into the Packers Hall of Fame in 2009.

John Brockington is the third-leading rusher in team history with 5,024 yards. And much of that yardage was piled up in his first three seasons, when he was NFL offensive rookie of the year (1971) and a three-time Pro Bowler (1971–73). A first-round draft pick in 1971, Brockington roared onto the scene, rushing for 1,105 yards his first season and 3,276 yards in his first three years. He teamed with fullback MacArthur Lane in 1972 to create a devastating backfield that led the Packers to the playoffs. But Lane was traded two years later, the offense took on a new look, and Brockington's numbers plummeted. After the first game of the 1977 season he was traded to the Kansas City Chiefs, and he retired after that season.

TACKLES

The Candidates

Forrest Gregg

Bob Skoronski

David Bakhtiari

Now we dive into the offensive line, where names converge, statistics don't exist, and impressions drive the conversation.

Who was a great tackle and who was the best guard? How do you rate a center and how do they make themselves stand out?

Their skills are often masked but their talents appreciated by the guys on the team.

FORREST GREGG

Let's be honest here. The best offensive lineman in the long and distinguished history of the Green Bay Packers is Forrest Gregg.

There are few, if any, who will argue that point. And while there have been some excellent to superb offensive linemen who have gotten in the trenches for the Packers, Gregg stands above them all.

Forrest Gregg in 1965
AP PHOTO/VERNON BIEVER

If he did not redefine the position and rewrite the job description for what it meant to be a tackle in the NFL, then he certainly perfected it.

He had the size—6-foot-4 and 250 pounds—as well as the agility, power, and technique to dominate the premier defensive linemen of his era. And he did so on a consistently superb basis.

SMU's Alvis Forrest Gregg was selected in the second round of the 1956 draft, spent 1957 in military service, took his spot at right tackle in 1958, and did not leave until 1970. That was a span of 188 straight games, which was a team record until a quarterback named Brett Favre came along.

And in that time, Gregg anchored an offensive line that won five NFL championships and established itself as the best the league had ever seen.

If casual football fans didn't really know what an offensive tackle did on a play-by-play basis, Gregg provided a tutorial.

"They say you don't get much recognition on the offensive line," Gregg said at his Hall of Fame induction. "But there is a lot of satisfaction if you know you're doing your job and the coaches know it. Our backs always knew they didn't make those long runs by themselves."

It is well known that Vince Lombardi was quoted as saying that Gregg was the best player he had ever coached. But the praise also came from some of the game's best players, including Dallas Cowboys defensive tackle Bob Lilly, the Minnesota Vikings' Carl Eller, and Merlin Olsen of the Los Angeles Rams.

His quarterback, Bart Starr, also raved.

"Where he separates himself from the other tackles is the way he hustles downfield for an extra block, even when the play goes the other way," Starr told Cliff Christl of Packers.com.

He was a critical part of Green Bay's five championships, and then in 1971 he joined the Dallas Cowboys, where he played a backup role for the Cowboys' Super Bowl–champion team.

He retired after that season and went on to a lengthy career as a coach—serving as an assistant with the San Diego Chargers and Cleveland Browns before becoming the Browns' head coach from 1975 to 1977.

He would also serve as the Cincinnati Bengals' head coach from 1980 to 1983, taking the Bengals to the Super Bowl in 1981, where they lost to the San Francisco 49ers.

After his friend and former teammate Bart Starr was fired by the Packers after the '83 season, Gregg was hired and the results were decidedly mixed.

He had always said he combined the coaching philosophies of Vince Lombardi and Tom Landry but he enjoyed little of their success.

"I played all those years for Vince Lombardi, and I learned a lot about football and about people," Gregg said in a 2016 interview with *Sports Illustrated*. "I tried to take what I could take from him and let it be mine. I did the same thing with Tom Landry. I was fortunate to play in Super Bowl VI with Tom, and Tom was totally different than Vince; you didn't have to worry about Tom yelling at you. He would find a way to tell you if you were doing something you weren't supposed to do."

But Gregg's 1980s Packers were not the 1960s Packers or the 1970s Cowboys. They were known to deliver cheap shots and play outside the bounds of sportsmanship. Worse, several Packers were cited for run-ins with the law.

In four seasons under Gregg, the Packers were 28-36 and he was fired after the '87 season.

His last stop was back at his alma mater, SMU, where he coached a team that was trying to recover after receiving a two-year "death penalty" from the NCAA.

He now lives in Colorado and suffers from Parkinson's disease, which he attributes to the years of constant collisions from football. But he has said often he would trade none of it.

Gregg was a nine-time Pro Bowler, a seven-time All-Pro, and a member of both the NFL's 75th Anniversary Team and the NFL's 1960s All-Decade Team. He was inducted into the Packers Hall of Fame and the Pro Football Hall of Fame in 1977.

BOB SKORONSKI

Quiet, efficient Bob Skoronski followed the old adage of letting his play do his talking.

"[Guards] Jerry Kramer and Fuzzy Thurston did all the talking," said Gary Knafelc, a teammate of Skoronski. "Bob didn't say a word. He just outblocked everybody."

Skoronski was another member of those legendary Packers teams of the 1960s—playing left tackle and, occasionally, center, and he was in the thick of all five Packers championships.

Knafelc said Skoronski often graded out higher after games than any other Packers offensive lineman—three of whom (Jim Ringo, Forrest Gregg, and Jerry Kramer) are in the Pro Football Hall of Fame.

Skoronski was a fifth-round draft pick in 1956 out of Indiana University. That draft, under head coach Lisle Blackbourn, was the first of several impactful drafts that would lead to the dominating Packers teams of the 1960s. Along with Skoronski, the Packers also selected Gregg and quarterback Bart Starr.

But Skoronski missed his first two seasons with the Packers due to required Air Force service. When he finally returned, he stepped into the left tackle position and never left the offensive line until he retired after the 1968 season.

Lombardi learned quickly how valuable and versatile Skoronski was and, when Ringo was traded prior to the 1964 season, Lombardi named Skoronski the team's offensive captain—a title he kept until he retired. To the players, it was the ultimate sign of respect from their coach.

"It's the greatest honor I've ever had," Skoronski said at the time. "You've got to play on this team to understand what it's like being a Packer."

Bob Skoronski

And he understood only too well. He just did his job quietly and effectively.

Consider one of the greatest games in NFL history—the 1967 NFL Championship known forever and always as the "Ice Bowl."

While Starr got credit for sneaking in for the game-winning touchdown over the Dallas Cowboys, and Kramer and, later, center Ken Bowman were credited with the decisive block, Skoronski was every bit as important.

Starr knew that if Skoronski did not block Dallas defensive end George Andrie, he would slide over and cut off the hole Starr was planning to slip through.

In the huddle he asked Skoronski if he could make that block, and Skoronski said simply, "Yes." To this day Starr believes Skoronski should be in the Pro Football Hall of Fame and likely would be if he hadn't been overshadowed by teammate Forrest Gregg.

Skoronski did earn one Pro Bowl berth and was inducted into the Packers Hall of Fame in 1976. His absence from the Pro Football Hall never bothered Skoronski, who knew playing for five championship teams was reward enough.

He died in October 2018 from complications from Alzheimer's disease.

David Bakhtiari

In the 2018 season, when very little went right for the Packers, especially on the offensive line, David Bakhtiari was a beacon of stability, durability, and quality.

A fourth-round pick of the Packers in 2013 from the University of Colorado, Bakhtiari was drafted as an insurance pick

David Bakhtiari in 2015
KYLE ENGMAN VIA WIKIMEDIA COMMONS

and backup for Bryan Bulaga, the Packers' first-round pick three years earlier, who was dealing with nagging injuries.

It proved to be an inspired selection, as during the Packers' annual "Family Night" preseason scrimmage that summer, Bulaga suffered a severe knee injury that would end his season. Bakhtiari, untested and all but unknown, stepped in and has never left. In fact, when Bulaga returned from his injury, he was moved to right tackle because of how well Bakhtiari had filled in.

As a left tackle, he is responsible for protecting the blind side of franchise quarterback Aaron Rodgers and he has done that superbly. And now Rodgers trusts him implicitly, even commenting that he has a chance to be a Hall of Fame tackle.

In his six seasons through 2018, Bakhtiari has already been named to one Pro Bowl and an alternate for two others. In 2018 he was tabbed by NFL observers as perhaps the major snub for a Pro Bowl berth despite having a 92.3 pass-blocking grade, the best among all tackles in the league. In fact, he has scored over 90 percent in the last three seasons. Interestingly enough, while he did not garner Pro Bowl accolades, he was named first-team All-Pro for the first time in his career.

Rodgers believes there is little Bakhtiari can't accomplish in his career.

"I think he has Hall of Fame potential," Rodgers said during the 2018 season. "He's an incredible player. He's been a rock for us. When he's over there, you feel really comfortable with him locking down pass rushers throughout the game. He's played through some injuries, he's had a fantastic season again, and obviously having him out there has been great."

Will he continue a performance that has made him one of the game's best? Only time will tell. But the initial evidence is there for all to see. He has made a name for himself, and for a team of Hall of Famers, there are few who doubt he belongs.

AND THE WINNERS ARE . . .

Forrest Gregg resides at one tackle spot. Any questions? He was the best in the business for 15 seasons, most of which saw the Packers dominating the NFL. He has been a Packers icon for decades and any list of the game's tackles is a farce if he's not mentioned.

But the other spot? That's worth some deep thinking. We're going out on a limb and selecting a player on the current roster as of the 2018 season. In his first six seasons with the Packers, **David Bakhtiari** has established himself as one of the top left tackles in the game and he's still in the prime of his career. If he stays healthy (never a certainty these days), he has a chance to find his name not only in the Packers Hall of Fame but, just maybe, in that hall in Canton, Ohio.

TACKLES WHO DID NOT MAKE THE CUT

Chad Clifton was a player Forrest Gregg would have liked both as a teammate and as a player. Quiet and solid and efficient and always ready to play, Clifton battled through injuries for years and always came out on the other side. As with many left tackles, Clifton waged his wars every week in relative anonymity, until of course a defensive end came crashing in on the quarterback. But Clifton, a second-round draft pick in 2000 from the University of Tennessee, did his job week in and week out, starting 160 of 165 games over his 11-year career in Green Bay.

A two-time Pro Bowler, Clifton is, unfortunately, best known for the incident early in his career that nearly *ended* that career. In a November 2002 game against the Tampa Bay Buccaneers in Tampa, quarterback Brett Favre threw an interception and Clifton, trailing the play by a good 15 yards, was watching it unfold when Bucs All-Pro defensive tackle Warren Sapp roared into Clifton with a devastating (and legal, according to the NFL) blindside block that brought gasps from the crowd and rage from Packers players. Clifton lay on the turf for 15 minutes, with a frightening numbness in his legs, before he was taken off on a stretcher with a severe hip injury that ended his season. Debate raged for weeks about the legality of the hit and about Sapp's response to it. But Clifton remained above the fray and concentrated instead on rehabbing his injury and getting back on the field. Clifton worked hard to get healthy and ready for the next season, and by the time the 2003 opener rolled around, he was in his familiar left tackle spot—and started all 16 games. He would go on to establish himself as an anchor on the Packers offensive line over the next eight years. The highlight for him was playing in Super Bowl XLV as Green Bay beat the Pittsburgh Steelers for its first Super Bowl title since 1996. In 2016 he was inducted into the Packers Hall of Fame.

To play for the Green Bay Packers was, almost literally, a dream come true for Marshfield, Wisconsin, native **Mark Tauscher**. Nothing came easily to Tauscher, who made the University of Wisconsin football team as a walk-on in 1995, played a backup role for two seasons, then moved in as the starting right tackle for the Badgers his final two seasons. In the 2000 NFL draft, Tauscher was a seventh-round pick and a long shot at best at making the team. But after an injury to longtime right tackle Earl Dotson, Tauscher stepped in and played for 11 seasons. His solid play and local ties made him a fan favorite, and in 2008 he was named the Packers' representative for the Walter Payton Man of the Year Award. He started in Super Bowl XLV in February 2011 and was released in July. He has remained in Wisconsin since. In 2018, another dream for the Wisconsin kid came true when he was inducted into the Packers Hall of Fame.

Packers fans everywhere remember that in 1993 Reggie White set the league on fire by signing a four-year, $16 million free agent deal that immediately put the Packers back on the NFL radar. Some 70 years earlier, **Howard "Cub" Buck** did something very much like it. Except, of course, the NFL did not yet exist. Buck had already established his reputation at the University of Wisconsin as one of the top college football players in the country and, after college, he signed up to play for the legendary Canton Bulldogs, joining the already famous Jim Thorpe on the team. Buck joined the Bulldogs in 1916 and remained with them until 1920, when they became part of the new American Professional Football Association. Then in 1921, not long before the APFA evolved into the National Football

League, the player-coach of the league's newest team, Curly Lambeau's Green Bay Packers, offered Buck the astounding sum of $100 per game. No one had ever seen anything like it. Buck went on to play for the Packers until 1925 and then coached at the University of Miami. He was inducted into the Packers Hall of Fame in 1977, still known as one the team's first "high-priced" purchases.

Ken Ruettgers was the Packers' first-round draft pick in 1985 and played so well that in 1989 he was named the team's offensive MVP from his left tackle position. Ruettgers started 140 of 156 games and suffered through some of the toughest times in team history. So when Mike Holmgren was named head coach in 1992, Ruettgers felt rejuvenated and played some of the best football of his career as the Packers rose to prominence. But early in the 1996 season, injuries caught up with him and he was placed on the Physically Unable to Perform list. It was the ultimate irony as the Packers won their first Super Bowl in 30 years and Ruettgers was on the sidelines. He retired after the season and was inducted into the Packers Hall of Fame in 2013.

GUARDS

The Candidates
Jerry Kramer
Mike Michalske
Fuzzy Thurston
Gale Gillingham

It's not quite so easy to select two guards, simply because as dominant as Forrest Gregg was at tackle, there have been a host of very talented guards who have played for the Packers over the decades. In fact, two are in the Pro Football Hall of Fame and another two should be.

But since we have room for only two, some superb players will be left out. It's a tough business.

JERRY KRAMER
If there is an ambassador for the Green Bay Packers and everything they are and have been, it is this man. He came out of Idaho as one the state's best athletes and arrived in Green Bay as a green, naive kid. A talented guard and a pretty good kicker, he was a fourth-round draft pick for a Packers organization that had been spinning its wheels for more than 20 years.

Donny Anderson (44) following the blocks of guards Gale Gillingham (68) and Jerry Kramer (64) in the Packers' 33-14 victory over the Oakland Raiders in Super Bowl II on January 14, 1968
AP PHOTO/VERNON BIEVER

And in his first season, under hopelessly overmatched head coach Ray McLean, it would get worse as the Packers posted their worst record ever—1-10-1.

Amazingly, though, on that disastrous team the pieces for a dynasty were already in place. Along with the rookie Kramer, who didn't play much that first season, was quarterback Bart Starr, linebacker Ray Nitschke, center Jim Ringo, fullback Jim Taylor, halfback Paul Hornung, and left tackle Forrest Gregg.

All that was needed were a few more players and a coach to take them in the right direction and make them believe in themselves.

Those parts arrived and so did the coach—a former New York Giants offensive coordinator named Vince Lombardi.

He was a coach who impacted everyone he came in contact with. But perhaps no one more than Kramer, who even decades later preaches the gospel of the "old man."

Lombardi was hard on Kramer because he knew he could be, and while he sometimes bristled at the criticism, often delivered in front of the entire team and in truly pungent fashion, Kramer also knew he was improving.

A story he has recounted many times is when he was sitting in front of his locker after an especially awful practice in which Lombardi questioned whether he could even play in the league. Kramer had his head in his hands when Lombardi came by and cupped his head affectionately.

"Jerry," he said, "you're a great player and you're going to be a star in this league."

Then he walked away.

"You have no idea how that made me feel," says Kramer, who gets emotional even these days telling the tale.

And he did become a star in this league.

For 10 seasons he anchored the Packers' right guard position and, along with left guard Fuzzy Thurston, formed the devastating pulling guard tandem that created the fearsome and feared "Packers Sweep."

Kramer brought an athleticism to the offensive line that was just coming into vogue in the league. Evidence of that is that in the 1962 NFL title game against the New York Giants in a cold, windy, and rainy Yankee Stadium. Kramer, a 250-pound guard, kicked three field goals that helped seal a 16–7 win.

A fourth-round draft pick in 1958 from the University of Idaho, Kramer had already proven he could overcome adversity.

Indeed, at age 15 he had been accidentally shot in his right arm by a shotgun and had to endure eight skin grafts.

Two years later, while he was chasing a calf on the family farm, an eight-inch piece of wood penetrated his groin and lodged near his spine. He also overcame numerous injuries on the football field, including a chipped vertebrae and damaged ankle ligaments. He also missed the entire 1964 season with a tumor on his liver.

But he persevered because he could not imagine disappointing Lombardi.

As good as he was as a player, Kramer was also a talented writer, and at the start of the 1967 season he was asked to keep a diary about the daily life of an NFL player and the team he played with. Cowritten with New York sportswriter Dick Schaap, the resulting book was called *Instant Replay* and it became a bestseller.

Kramer knew he was nearing the end of his career anyway, and the thought of being an author was appealing to him. He would go on to write another eight books and is still working on a script about Lombardi, the man who made such an impact on his life.

Kramer has joked often about trying to retire, but failing at it. Instead, he has spent his life since his playing days as a professional Packer. He has done thousands of speaking engagements and played hundreds of rounds of golf. And all he has had to do is be Jerry Kramer.

For a long time, the only blank spot on his resume was his absence from the Pro Football Hall of Fame. Whether Hall voters had Packers weariness or disliked his ability to shine the spotlight a little too hotly on himself, Kramer always came up short.

In recent years, Kramer had made peace with the fact that a spot in Canton was not to be, even though he was a four-time All-Pro, a three-time Pro Bowler, and a member of the NFL's 50th Anniversary Team; was named to the Packers' All-Century Team and All-Modern Era Team; and was inducted into the Packers Hall of Fame in 1975.

Finally, in August 2017, the Hall of Fame's senior committee named Kramer one of the finalists for induction. And in February 2018 he was selected, 50 years after he retired.

He began his induction speech in typical fashion.

"Thank you, thank you, thank you, thank you. I could say 'thank you' the rest of the evening and not get it done," he said. "This is a wonderful moment."

And long overdue.

MIKE MICHALSKE

His given name was August, but over time he was simply "Iron Mike" because . . . why not? Michalske was another from the era that saw players compete on both offense and defense (it was a league rule in the early NFL, but it likely would have been hard to find players who didn't want to do both).

And Michalske, tough and quick and agile, relished the opportunity, often playing on the line for the entire 60 minutes. He was a good defensive lineman but he was a better offensive guard, perhaps the best the NFL would see in its first 30 years, and was lauded years later by his teammate, and halfback, Johnny "Blood" McNally.

"He was as great as any football player Green Bay ever had," McNally said, as quoted by Packers.com. "He had very fast reflexes. He would start moving before his opponents.

That was his chief asset, besides his tremendous fighting spirit."

Michalske got his start with the old New York Yankees in 1926 when they were a member of the American Football League. Then he played for the Yankees the next two seasons when they joined the NFL. When the Yankees folded in 1929, he signed with the Packers, making a good team even better.

He was part of three straight championships (in 1929, 1930, and 1931) and retired in 1936 to become basketball coach and an assistant football coach at Lafayette College. He came back in 1937 to play one more season (and serve as line coach), but injuries forced him out again and he retired for good to begin a lengthy career as a coach.

Michalske was inducted into the Pro Football Hall of Fame in 1964 and the Packers Hall of Fame in 1970. He also was named to the NFL's All-Decade Team for the 1920s, was a five-time All-Pro, and was selected to the Packers' All-Time Team and the Packers' All-Iron Man Era Team.

Fuzzy Thurston

For nearly a decade, the guard tandem of Frederick "Fuzzy" Thurston and Jerry Kramer were inseparable. Indeed, football fans of that era could hardly say one of their names without saying the other.

And through the run of five championships, Thurston and Kramer may well have been the most recognizable linemen in the NFL.

Good-natured, optimistic, funny, and highly quotable, Thurston backed up his personality with exceptional play. One training camp, a reporter asked Thurston why the Packers kept winning championships.

He smiled and said, "Kramer is one reason and you're looking at the other." When asked how he kept warm during the infamous "Ice Bowl" in 1967 when the temperature dipped to 20 below zero, he responded that he drank about 10 vodkas. And no one doubted him.

Thurston, like several other Packers from the 1960s, found a circuitous route to Green Bay. Originally drafted by the Philadelphia Eagles in 1956, he played little and then took

FRED THURSTON
GREEN BAY PACKERS   GUARD

Fred "Fuzzy" Thurston's Topps Card
THE TOPPS COMPANY VIA WIKIMEDIA COMMONS

two years off to fulfill his military requirement in the army. He returned in 1958 to play for the Baltimore Colts, who beat the New York Giants in overtime for the NFL title that is still known as the Greatest Game Ever Played. (Thurston was in on a handful of plays.)

In 1959 he was traded to the Packers, whose new coach had been the Giants' offensive coordinator the year before—Vince Lombardi. And like so many other players, Thurston's life and career changed.

He teamed up with Kramer to fashion the two-man pulling guard wrecking crew that made up the "Packers Sweep." And it was next to unstoppable even though defenses knew it was coming.

Thurston was part of all five Packers championships and is one of just three players in NFL history to play on six championship teams (ironically, the other two are also Packers—Forrest Gregg and Herb Adderley).

Injuries caught up to Thurston in 1967, and he was on the sideline for most of the "Ice Bowl" as the youngster Gale Gillingham took his place at left guard. When Lombardi stepped down as head coach after Super Bowl II, Thurston retired as well.

A Wisconsin native, he remained in the Green Bay area the rest of his life, owning several restaurants and bars in that time. He was an All-Pro once and was inducted into the Packers Hall of Fame in 1975, and there was a push for many years to get him into the Pro Football Hall of Fame.

He died in 2014 from the effects of Alzheimer's disease and cancer.

GALE GILLINGHAM

In a way, Gale Gillingham marked the beginning of the end of the Packers NFL dynasty that was the 1960s.

A first-round draft pick in 1966, Gillingham slipped seamlessly into the Packers' loaded lineup and ended up playing until 1976, when the golden age of Green Bay Packers football was only a pleasant memory to many fans.

He was a superb guard who now has usurped his colleague Jerry Kramer (inducted in 2018) as the best player not in the Pro Football Hall of Fame. But he was also a new breed of offensive lineman who combined his size—6-foot-3 and 260 pounds—with a quickness and agility that would be required in the emerging NFL.

Kramer remembers watching Gillingham as a rookie and saying to him that he (Kramer) was no longer the fastest offensive lineman on the team.

"The kid could really move," Kramer recalled. "Plus he was as strong as an ox."

Packers running back John Brockington related the same impression to Packers historian Cliff Christl.

"He was a beast," Brockington recalled. "Gilly was a weightlifter and he pounded those weights. He was something else. Physical and fast. Put somebody ordinary over [Gillingham] and the guy had no chance. Gilly was going to pound him to death."

Gillingham served a year's apprenticeship behind Thurston at left guard in 1966 and then burst on the scene the following season, in part because Thurston suffered a knee injury in training camp. In truth, Lombardi had seen how dominant Gillingham could be and had Thurston not been hurt, Gillingham likely would have taken over as the starter anyway.

Yet to Thurston's credit, despite the writing on the wall, he tutored the youngster in ways only a veteran NFL lineman could. And Gillingham always credited Thurston for helping him learn the game a lot faster.

Gillingham played left guard through 1968, and when Kramer retired he moved over to right guard; all told, he was a Pro Bowler three times and an All-Pro four times.

But in 1972, Packers coach Dan Devine, facing a dearth of defensive tackles due to injury, decided it was a good idea to move his All-Pro guard, Gillingham, to defensive tackle, a move that stunned teammates, fans, and, more importantly, Gillingham.

"I don't know what he was thinking," Gillingham said years later.

Two games into the season, Gillingham injured his knee and was lost for the rest of the season that saw Green Bay win its first division title in five years.

Devine came to his senses and returned Gillingham to where he belonged the next season. He once again earned Pro Bowl and All-Pro berths in 1973 and 1974.

But, unhappy with where the Packers were headed, battling injuries, and in a full-blown war with his line coach, Leon McLaughlin, Gillingham demanded a trade or he would sit out the 1975 season. The Packers did not trade him.

"I had no faith in the line coach and didn't fit into the system," he told Martin Hendricks of the *Milwaukee Journal Sentinel* years later.

He returned in 1976, but playing under his old teammate Bart Starr did nothing to rekindle Gillingham's fire. And after a 5-9 season, he'd had enough and retired.

"The losing killed me," he told the *Journal Sentinel*. "I was burned out and beat up both mentally and physically."

He was a six-time All-Pro and a five-time Pro Bowler and was inducted into the Packers Hall of Fame in 1982.

And while his induction into the Pro Football Hall seems unlikely now, the Professional Football Researchers Association named Gillingham to its Hall of Very Good, Class of 2016. Ironically, his mentor, Fuzzy Thurston, is in that hall, too.

In 2011, while lifting weights at his home in Minnesota, Gillingham died of a heart attack. He was just 67.

And the Winners Are . . .

Tough calls here since all are worthy of taking their place on this team. But the first spot goes to **Jerry Kramer** for two reasons—he was a superb guard for a long time, and he has kept the legend of Vince Lombardi and the mystique of the Green Bay Packers teams of the 1960s alive for new generations to enjoy and understand.

The other spot? Running buddy Fuzzy Thurston, or Mike Michalske, perhaps the first great offensive lineman in team history, would be excellent choices.

But the selection here is **Gale Gillingham**, who slipped in to replace the injured Thurston at left guard and the Packers never missed a beat on the line. Later, Gillingham moved to the other side to take over for the veteran Kramer and he was one of the league's best. When he retired in 1976, he was the last starter from the Super Bowl teams still playing. And, as with so many other players from those championship years, his devotion to the Packers continued until his death.

Guards Who Did Not Make the Cut

Marco Rivera was a sixth-round draft pick in 1996 and was part of two Super Bowl teams (though he was inactive the entire 1996 season and was mostly a special teamer in 1997). But after two seasons of playing in the World League of American Football, Rivera developed into a top-notch lineman, first as a left guard and then on the right side. Once he won the starting job in 1998, he never missed a game through his final season in Green Bay in 2004. And despite playing with a bad back and damaged knees, he was a three-time Pro Bowl selection (2002–04) and a two-time All-Pro (2003 and 2004). He also received the Ed Block Courage Award in 2004. In 2005 he signed a five-year, $20 million free agent deal with the Dallas Cowboys, but physical woes cut his time short and he retired after the 2006 season. Inducted into the Packers Hall of Fame 2011, he moved into coaching and lives in Dallas.

At 6-foot-1, 245 pounds, there was nothing to suggest the nickname of **Paul Engebretsen**—which happened to be "Tiny." He bounced around in the early 1930s, playing for the Chicago Cardinals and Bears as well as the Pittsburgh Pirates and Brooklyn Dodgers before he was traded to the Packers in 1934, where he found a home for the next nine seasons. He was one of the league's top guards, earning all-league honors in 1936 and 1939. He was also one of the NFL's best kickers, leading the league in extra points in 1939 with 18. He scored 100 points in his career, hitting 15 of 28 field goals and 55 of 62 extra points. After retiring two games into the 1941 season, he became a Packers scout and eventually got into coaching. He was inducted into the Packers Hall of Fame in 1978. He died in 1979 in his native Iowa.

Josh Sitton was selected in the fourth round of the 2008 draft and went on to a solid, versatile, and, ultimately, controversial career with the Packers. He played every game at right guard in the 2009 and '10 seasons and, after five years there, he shifted to left guard, where he played his remaining three seasons. He even filled in at left tackle due to injuries to other players. He was named to four Pro Bowls and was a first-team All-Pro in 2014 and a two-time alternate, in 2013 and 2015. But he was critical of the Packers' offensive game plan in a playoff loss to the Arizona Cardinals in 2015, and in the final cutdown before the 2016 season, in a stunning move, he was released. He signed with the rival Chicago Bears, earning one more Pro Bowl berth before he was released in 2018. He signed with the Miami Dolphins but an injury ended his season. He maintains he has no ill will toward the Packers or how his release was handled.

CENTER

The Candidates

Frank Winters
Jim Ringo
Larry McCarren

They played with a quiet efficiency, perhaps understanding that as they anchored the middle of an offensive line where mayhem was all around them, it was more important to do the job well because of all that was at stake. After all, is there anything more elemental in football than the center-quarterback exchange? And the one time in a thousand opportunities it doesn't go off smoothly, does it ever not result in disaster?

But these three finalists, again spanning different eras, were the best at what they did—even if few outside their sphere knew just how difficult their job was.

FRANK WINTERS

Exhibit A is Frank Winters. He labored in the kind of obscurity that centers are supposed to accept as part of the job. It is a thankless, brutal, painful position that receives little recognition, and even the centers who do receive honors often don't know what they did that was any better than any of the other centers in the league.

And no one understood this better than Winters, who played 16 seasons in the NFL, 11 with the Packers, and was known by fans everywhere as perhaps one of quarterback Brett Favre's best friends on the team.

He was not Favre's only center, but he is the one most aligned with the mercurial quarterback, the center who knew Favre so well, he could predict what he was going to do even if Favre didn't. But more to the point, Winters was a journeyman, a center who bounced from several clubs before finding his place with a Packers team that was on the threshold of something truly special. Winters always appreciated his long career and never, ever took it for granted.

But he made the most of everything he got in the NFL, triggering one of the league's best offenses while working with a quarterback whose like will never be seen again.

The two men also became close friends, drawn together in 1992 as newcomers to a rebuilding Packers team. Winters had already played in the league for five seasons—two in Cleveland, one with the New York Giants, and two with the Kansas City Chiefs—when he was signed as a free agent by the Packers.

They were a mismatched pair and polar opposites in almost every way. Favre was a country boy from Mississippi who was brash and brimming with confidence and, yes, was the cornerstone for a Packers renaissance. Winters was a city kid from Union City, New Jersey, another in a long line of faceless offensive linemen who was hoping just to remain in the league.

But they clicked immediately and over time became almost inseparable. They played golf together. They fished together. They celebrated and commiserated together. Winters was with Favre when the quarterback checked himself into a drug rehab clinic prior to the 1996 season. Five months later, when

Winters's brother John died unexpectedly prior to the Super Bowl, Favre comforted him.

And on the field, they were of one mind—the quarterback calling the plays and the center orchestrating the offensive line that would protect him.

The two played together through thick and thin, but when coach Mike Holmgren left after the 1998 season to become general manager and head coach of the Seattle Seahawks, Winters could feel a change coming. Still, he joined many veteran teammates in believing Holmgren left too soon because these Packers were still built to win Super Bowls.

The Packers sagged under first-year coach Ray Rhodes, who was fired after one season, and began a revitalization under his replacement, Mike Sherman. But Winters had waged war in the trenches for more than a decade and the wear and tear were catching up to him.

"The game takes a toll," he said, adding that after the 2000 season he told Sherman he was going to retire, but Sherman convinced him to return for one more year.

In fact, Winters played two more seasons before he was released prior to the 2003 season.

Winters earned his lone Pro Bowl berth in 1996. When he was inducted into the Packers Hall of Fame in 2008, Favre was there to pat him on his belly and introduce him. Winters was also on hand when Favre went into the Pro Football Hall of Fame in 2016.

JIM RINGO

A seventh-round draft pick in 1953 from Syracuse University, Jim Ringo was, at 210 pounds, a small offensive lineman even back then.

He had been dealing with such perceptions for years, and he knew that quickness and agility and intelligence could make up for his other shortcomings. And over an 11-year career in Green Bay, Ringo developed into one of the greatest centers the league has ever seen.

But it almost never came to pass.

When Ringo reported to Packers training camp as a rookie, he was stunned by the size and quality of the players and was convinced he could not measure up. So early in camp, certain he had no shot of making an NFL team (even a mediocre one like the Packers), he went back home to New Jersey.

"But I wasn't welcome there," he said later. "They didn't like a quitter. They said, 'You should at least try,' and so I went back."

He beat back challenge after challenge, took over the center position, and never let it go.

Unfortunately for Ringo, the first five years of his career were played in relative obscurity and for, arguably, the worst stretch of teams the franchise has ever seen. Under four coaches—Gene Ronzani, Ray McLean, Hugh Devore, and Lisle Blackbourn—the Packers never had a winning record.

Still, Ringo performed at a high level, earning Pro Bowl and All-Pro berths in 1957 and 1958.

But, in what became a familiar refrain, upon Vince Lombardi's hiring in 1959, everything changed not only for the team but for individual players.

Lombardi saw Ringo as the lone veteran talent on his offensive line and his idea was simple but effective—he would make Ringo the pivot of the line that would produce one of the most devastating running games the NFL had ever seen.

"The reason Ringo's the best in the league is because he's quick and he's smart," Lombardi once said, as reported on

ProFootballHOF.com. "He runs the offensive line, calls the blocks, and he knows what every lineman does on every play."

Ringo made it even clearer.

"All I know is [pro football] was a means of survival for myself. When I went on the field, I went out with the intention of excelling."

And so he did, becoming an integral part of the Packers' NFL titles in 1961 and 1962.

Ringo was at the top of his game and a perennial all-star but starting to reach a point in his career where his skills were not what they once were. So following the 1963 season, in a story that over time has been embellished with fact and myth, Ringo came to Lombardi accompanied by an agent (almost unheard of in those days), seeking a raise.

Reportedly furious at Ringo's brazen request, the coach/general manager excused himself and came back a few minutes later to tell Ringo he'd been traded to the Philadelphia Eagles.

It was a wonderful story and Lombardi did little to correct it because he liked the fact it offered a stark example that coaches were still in charge.

Over the years, it became clear that Ringo had sought a trade so he could be closer to his New Jersey home. Ringo continued his All-Pro career with the Eagles and retired after the 1967 season.

He went immediately into coaching, serving as offensive line coach and offensive coordinator with the Buffalo Bills, New England Patriots, Chicago Bears, Los Angeles Rams, and New York Jets through 1988.

He was a 10-time Pro Bowler and a nine-time All-Pro, was a member of the NFL's All-Decade Team for the 1960s, and was inducted into the Packers Hall of Fame in 1974 and the

Pro Football Hall of Fame in 1981. He died in 2007, just two days shy of his 76th birthday.

LARRY MCCARREN

In the mold of Jim Ringo, McCarren was there every week, playing the game the way it was meant to be played.

A 12th-round draft pick in 1973 out of the University of Illinois, McCarren took over as the starting center late that season and played a remarkable 168 straight games, still the fourth-longest streak in team history.

"It was a different game then," he said. "You played with injuries."

And he proved that fact time and again, including 1980, when McCarren had hernia surgery in training camp and was still far from 100 percent when the season opened against the rival Bears. Coach Bart Starr, aware that McCarren hadn't missed a start since 1974, planned to put McCarren in for the first play, keep the streak alive, and then remove him so he could finish healing.

But after the first play McCarren waved off his replacement and remained in the game.

He also played through a broken hand and, one time, after his family had been overcome by carbon monoxide fumes early one morning, still managed to be in the lineup later in the day.

"It's what you had to do," he said.

Never flashy, he rarely received the accolades he deserved, though he was a two-time Pro Bowler, in 1982 and 1983. But McCarren was consistent and durable, earning the nickname "Rock," and he helped trigger some of the most prolific offensive teams in team history.

Not surprisingly, one of the highlights of McCarren's career came in that still legendary 1983 Monday night game against the defending Super Bowl champion Washington Redskins.

Anchoring a completely revamped offensive line in which none of the players was at the position they were most comfortable with (except McCarren), the Packers piled up 473 total yards in a 48–47 victory.

McCarren played in an era when the Packers produced some prolific offensive performances. Unfortunately for him, those great offenses didn't get a lot of help from the defense. So in McCarren's 12-year career, he participated in just two playoff games and his teams posted a combined 71-99-5 record.

But McCarren was always there and his play always caught the attention of rivals.

Chicago Bears linebacker Tom Hicks recalled how McCarren never said much but went out and did his job game in and game out.

Quarterback Lynn Dickey agreed.

"He's the toughest player I've ever been around," he said.

Asked about his career, McCarren shrugged.

"I viewed myself as a worker bee," he said.

But he couldn't play forever, and toward the end of the 1984 season a pinched nerve in his neck finally forced him to the sidelines. He tried to come back in 1985 but it was obvious he couldn't, and he finally retired.

After football McCarren stayed in Wisconsin and has worked on TV and radio since. He joined the Packers' radio network in 1995, teaming with Jim Irwin and Max McGee on broadcasts, and when Wayne Larrivee came in as the Packers' play-by-play announcer in 1999, McCarren stepped in as the color analyst.

McCarren was inducted into the Packers Hall of Fame in 1992, calling it "a rather humbling experience."

AND THE WINNER IS . . .

You have to go with the numbers here. Though considered undersized, even for the NFL of the 1950s, **Jim Ringo** was the best center in the league for a long time. The only smudge on his record is that, early in his career, he played for some awful Packers teams. But once Vince Lombardi appeared on the scene, everything changed. Versatile and smart and durable, Ringo was a 10-time Pro Bowler and a Hall of Famer who played 126 games for the Packers.

CENTERS WHO DID NOT MAKE THE CUT

In time, current Packers center **Corey Linsley** may take over the top spot. But not yet. He still needs to put in a few more years and garner a few more accolades. But the Ohio State product, and fifth-round draft pick in 2014, has shown the kind of toughness and skill that is a hallmark of Packers centers over the years. He was thrust in as the starting center in 2014 during his rookie training camp when designated starter J. C. Tretter suffered an injury. He took over and played like a seasoned veteran and has held the position since. In fact, through the 2018 season he has snapped the ball 2,484 straight times—all 1,074 snaps in 2018, all 1,047 snaps in 2017, and the final 363 snaps of the 2016 season. How's that for durability?

Ken Bowman, a cerebral and iconoclastic University of Wisconsin product, battled injury and constant challenges to his starting job and also found time to earn his law degree in the off-season. Bowman, an eighth-round draft pick in 1964, won the starting center job despite challenges from three other players. A chronic shoulder injury forced him out of the lineup in 1966 before he won his job back in 1967. He is best known, especially in recent years, for helping throw the key block in the "Ice Bowl" that allowed Bart Starr to score the winning touchdown. Jokingly, he has said he gave more credit to Jerry Kramer because Kramer was older. Politically active, Bowman was arrested in 1974 during an NFL player protest and he was subsequently released by the Packers, signing with the Hawaiians of the World Football League, which folded a few weeks later. He completed his law degree and went on to become a special magistrate in Arizona. He was inducted into the Packers Hall of Fame in 1981.

TIGHT END

The Candidates

Paul Coffman

Ron Kramer

There have been some very good tight ends in Packers history, and it's a position that has evolved for the Packers, as it has for many other teams. For many years a tight end was considered just another offensive lineman who could catch the occasional pass. But in the 1960s it became more than that, and the Packers were at the forefront of the change.

Maybe that's why for our all-star team there are just two tight ends who fit as candidates. One led the evolution from blocker to receiver and the other transformed the position into a serious offensive weapon. We don't discount other talented tight ends—such as Marv Fleming, Rich McGeorge, Ed West, Jackie Harris, and others. But our two finalists redefined the position.

PAUL COFFMAN

He was never supposed to be an NFL tight end. But in the proverbial example of being in the right place at the right time, Paul Coffman found himself as a centerpiece of a high-powered

Packers offense and one of the best offensive talents the franchise has ever seen.

In his eight seasons with the Packers, Coffman caught 322 passes, averaged more than 13 yards a catch, scored 39 touchdowns, and was named to three Pro Bowls.

And it almost didn't happen.

It was one of those serendipitous moments in the spring of 1978 when Coffman, who had finished his eligibility at Kansas State ("It was one of the worst college programs in the country," Coffman said), went along to a Packers draft tryout scheduled for his teammate and friend, linebacker Gary Spani.

Coffman asked Packers assistant coach John Meyer if he'd take a look at him, too, and after a workout Meyer came away impressed with Coffman's ability to catch everything thrown his way.

In that spring's draft, Coffman wasn't selected but Meyer never forgot what the unknown tight end had shown him. And in a second piece of good fortune, the Packers found themselves without enough tight ends during training camp. Coach Bart Starr asked Meyer if he knew of any they could sign, and Meyer told him about Coffman.

"He won't make the team," Meyer told Starr, "but he won't embarrass us either."

Coffman survived training camp and the final cuts but played little that season.

That next season, Coffman stepped in to replace longtime starter Rich McGeorge, catching 56 passes (which would be his career high) and scoring four touchdowns. He also set what was at the time a team record for receptions by a tight end.

Through 1985 he never caught fewer than 42 passes for the Packers (except in the strike-shortened nine-game 1982 season) and was easily the first great offensive threat at tight end in team history.

He wasn't able to showcase his talents that often to a national audience, as in his eight seasons in Green Bay, the Packers managed just one winning record and two playoff games.

Bart Starr was fired after the 1984 season and replaced by another former Packer, Forrest Gregg. Coffman continued to put to up good numbers in his two seasons with Gregg, including 49 receptions and six touchdowns in 1985.

But prior to the '86 season, Coffman met with Gregg, who told the tight end there were two choices facing him as Gregg sought to rebuild the roster.

Gregg, who was looking to make the Packers younger, told Coffman that the Packers were either going to trade him to the Buffalo Bills or cut him (the Kansas City Chiefs had agreed to pick him up). Coffman was stunned, but since the Chiefs were interested and he was from Missouri anyway, he decided to accept being released.

That's when Gregg said that Coffman was now Kansas City's concern. It was a remark that stung Coffman but he knew he had never, ever given the Packers any problems. It was then he knew it was time to move.

Incredibly, quarterback Lynn Dickey was cut the same day, and Coffman recalled how the two Kansas State grads and friends were driving back to the Packers facility to return playbooks when Green Bay police pulled them over for speeding.

The police recognized both men and they told the cops what had happened.

"They couldn't believe it," Coffman said. "They radioed in and found out it was true. They let us go."

Coffman spent two seasons with the Chiefs and one in Minnesota before retiring.

He returned to Kansas City and still lives there, and three decades later he remains the Packers' all-time leader for receptions by a tight end.

He was inducted into the Packers Hall of Fame in 1994.

RON KRAMER

There may have been no better athlete to ever play tight end for the Packers than Ron Kramer. At the University of Michigan, he was a star in basketball, track, and, of course, football, where he was an All-American.

In 1957 he was the second of two first-round draft picks by Green Bay—the first was Paul Hornung, the Heisman Trophy winner from Notre Dame—with Kramer following three selections later.

Those two would go on to become close friends as well as crucial pieces to the Packers teams of the 1960s. But in those early years there was nothing to suggest that Kramer had found anything special in Green Bay. After all, he had played at Michigan and in a stadium that held more fans than the city of Green Bay's population. Going to Green Bay, he said, was nothing special.

And the teams he played for were equally sorry. The 1957 Packers were 3-9 in coach Lisle Blackbourn's last season. The next year, Ray McLean's only season as head coach, Green Bay was 1-10-1. Fortunately for Kramer, he missed that season due to military service. But when he returned, there was a new coach named Vince Lombardi.

"He was very convincing," Kramer told the *Flint Journal* in 1994. "He told us how good we could be."

And Lombardi was right.

Hornung's role changed under Lombardi and so did Kramer's. He was now able to get out into patterns, use his wondrous athleticism, and make plays downfield. He was also a key, and underrated, part of the blocking scheme that made up the "Packers Sweep."

Kramer flourished under Lombardi, catching two touchdown passes in the Packers' 37–0 NFL Championship win over the New York Giants in 1961 and earning All-Pro and Pro Bowl honors in 1962.

He was part of two NFL championship teams and he knew the Packers were capable of even more. But he also knew there was more to life than football and in 1965, facing family issues in Michigan that required him to be there, he played out his option and signed with the Detroit Lions.

It always bothered Kramer that people believed Lombardi was finished with him. But he said that was never true. A Michigan native, he simply wanted to be closer to his family and a move to the Lions made perfect sense.

He left Green Bay with 170 receptions and 15 touchdowns and averaged more than 15 yards a catch. But he also left a Packers team that went on to win three more championships. Kramer insisted he had no regrets.

He played three forgettable seasons in Detroit before retiring after the 1967 season. He remained in Michigan and ran several businesses. He was inducted into the Packers Hall of Fame in 1975 and named a member of the NFL's 50th Anniversary Team.

He died of a heart attack in 2010 at the age of 76.

And the Winner Is . . .

We cheated a little here because, upon reflection and analysis of the position, to make this all-star team required something special. And Ron Kramer and Paul Coffman were the only two who met that requirement. Either would be a great representative in this battle between two tight ends who did their jobs superbly but in very different ways and in very different eras.

Paul Coffman was the epitome of the tight end who was first and foremost an offensive weapon. Ron Kramer was a blocker who could catch the football. Both were excellent athletes and both, frankly, could be right at home in today's NFL. Kramer, however, was a key piece to two NFL championships, whereas Coffman played for decidedly less successful Packers teams. Does that matter? Maybe.

Another tough choice but the nod, due to his pure offensive production, is **Paul Coffman**.

Tight Ends Who Did Not Make the Cut

What might have been had **Jermichael Finley** stayed healthy. The University of Texas product had everything to take his place as the greatest tight end in team history. Size, speed, great athleticism, a terrific ability to run routes, and a confidence that bordered on cocky. When he was healthy, he was an impossible matchup for rival defenses and the most dominant offensive weapon the Packers had. But injuries dogged the 2008 third-round draft pick nearly his entire six-year career in Green Bay. Indeed, he played a full season only twice, and it was a serious neck injury early in the 2013 season that ultimately ended his career. Had he stayed healthy, he would have broken every team tight end record and likely would have moved to the top of this list. In just 70 games, he caught 223 passes and scored 20 touchdowns.

Mark Chmura was another key piece of the Holmgren-Wolf rebuild of the Packers in the 1990s. A sixth-round draft pick from Boston College in 1992, he was a classic big-body tight end—6-foot-5, 250 pounds—who was a terrific blocker and a great possession receiver and who grew to be a favorite target of quarterback Brett Favre. Injuries hampered much of his seven years in Green Bay, but he still caught 188 passes and scored 17 touchdowns and was named to three Pro Bowls. He was inducted into the Packers Hall of Fame in 2010.

A first-round draft pick in 2000, **Bubba Franks** was another of those big, strong, athletic tight ends who, like Chmura, became a favorite target of Favre, especially when he needed a quick outlet to a receiver. Sure-handed and fast, he was an excellent receiver who played just below the radar, even though he was a three-time Pro Bowler. He caught 262 passes and scored 32 touchdowns.

Ed West gets recognition for laboring 11 seasons (1984–94) with the Packers, through some very bad times and some pretty good ones. In fact, he had some of his best seasons late in his Packers career, actually setting his career high in receptions with 31 in 1994—his last season with the team. He finished with 202 receptions and 25 touchdowns and should be in the Packers Hall of Fame but, as of 2019, is not.

WIDE RECEIVERS

The Candidates
Don Hutson
Sterling Sharpe
Donald Driver
James Lofton
Jordy Nelson

It is impossible to name just two receivers for this all-star team given the wealth of talent of these candidates. So, given that fact, as well as the reality that today's NFL employs three wide receivers (at least) in most offensive sets, three receivers will be part of this team.

The Packers had perhaps the game's first great receiver, and over the years, no matter their result on the scoreboard, quality receivers have always found their way to Green Bay.

But even with naming three to our team, there will be choices here that some may not understand. Bear with us and the reasoning used should make the selections clear. Then again, maybe not.

DON HUTSON

It would, quite simply, be impossible to leave out one of the greatest players not only in Packers history, but in the history of the NFL. His name can still be found in the league record books 70 years after he left the game, and even if that wasn't the case, his impact on the forward pass and receiving changed the game.

Clark Shaughnessy, who coached more than 50 years on both the pro and college levels and was known as one of the game's great football minds, had high praise for Hutson back in 1943.

"In the years to come whenever forward-pass catching is mentioned, one name will always be mentioned first—Don Hutson, without a doubt the greatest pass catcher the game of football has ever known and probably the greatest it will ever know," he said. "No one but Superman could perform the feats Don Hutson has performed in catching passes."

At 6-foot-1 and 180 pounds and possessing great quickness, agility, and, of course, speed, Hutson burst onto the pro football scene in 1935 out of the University of Alabama, eventually earning the nickname "the Alabama Antelope."

In the days before the pro football draft, college players could sign wherever they wanted and Hutson signed with both the Packers and Brooklyn Dodgers—forcing league president Joe Carr to decide who held his rights.

The story goes that Carr picked the Packers because their contract with Hutson had the earlier postmark, and after the decision was made, Packers coach Curly Lambeau immediately signed the star end to the richest contract in team history—$300 per game.

Don Hutson

That deal paid off almost immediately when, on the first play of the second game of the season, Hutson hauled in an 83-yard touchdown pass from Arnie Herber as Green Bay beat the Bears, 7–0.

In a very real sense, that play showed that the NFL would never be the same. The forward pass, which was still viewed as little more than a novelty by some teams, was now a viable and decisive offensive weapon.

And Hutson would lead that onslaught.

Over 11 seasons in Green Bay, first with Herber at quarterback and then with his buddy Cecil Isbell throwing the ball, Hutson caught 488 passes and scored a remarkable 99 touchdowns, an NFL record that stood for more than 50 years.

"Hutson is the only man who can feint in three directions at once," cracked Philadelphia Eagles coach Greasy Neale at the time.

Between 1940 and 1942, Isbell and Hutson, who developed their chemistry by perfecting pass patterns during lunch hour on the parking lot of the factory they worked at in the off-season, teamed up to produce 34 touchdowns, including 17 in 1942. In one game against the Detroit Lions, Hutson scored 29 points; after his retirement in 1945, he owned 19 NFL records.

His accolades were lengthy and impressive, including being named a charter member of the Pro Football Hall of Fame in 1963. He was also an eight-time All-Pro, led the league in receiving yards seven times, and was the leading receiver eight times; additionally, he was a member of the NFL's 75th Anniversary Team.

His number 14 was retired by the team. He was inducted into the Packers Hall of Fame in 1972, and the Packers' $4 million indoor training facility, opened in 1994, was named the Don Hutson Center.

Hutson, who was also a member of the team's board of directors for years, died in 1997 at the age of 84, still revered as one of the great Packers of all time.

STERLING SHARPE

If Don Hutson is remembered by Packers fans with fondness and reverence, Sterling Sharpe is remembered with a bemused shake of the head.

Sharpe suffered fools not at all and played football because it was his job and because he was very, very good at it. He is famous for his decision as a rookie to stop speaking with the media, something he swears started off as a joke but then became cemented into a career-long standoff. But that was fine with Sharpe, who insisted years later that he never had anything he needed to tell the media anyway.

Irascible and unknowable and completely comfortable with it all, he could infuriate teammates and fans one minute but inspire awe the next by playing through the kind of injuries that would sideline other players.

Sharpe was Green Bay's first-round draft pick in 1988 for first-year coach Lindy Infante and caught 55 passes—not bad for a rookie. But he also dropped an inordinate number of balls, which the local media were only too happy to point out.

Sick of the criticism, he decided one day to stop answering questions, and he correlates that radio silence to his improved play over the years. Indeed, in 1989 he caught 90 passes and there was no looking back.

His performance took another step up in 1992 when Mike Holmgren brought his possession offense to Green Bay and Brett

Favre delivered the ball. In fact, Sharpe caught Favre's first-ever Packers TD pass in that unforgettable 1992 debut against the Cincinnati Bengals. It was also Sharpe, playing with such badly injured ribs he could barely breathe, who hauled in a 42-yard pass that set up Favre's winning TD toss, launching a legend.

Sharpe set a league record with 108 receptions and 1,461 yards that season and he did it again in 1993, catching 112 passes for 1,274 yards.

In 1994 he caught 94 balls with an NFL-best 18 touchdowns, including four against the Dallas Cowboys on a nationally televised Thanksgiving Day game.

His performance on the field was undeniable. It was the off-the-field stuff that drove people crazy. For example, the day before the 1994 season opener against Minnesota, Sharpe told the team he would not play because he was unhappy with his contract.

It was viewed by many teammates as a selfish and unproductive stunt that damaged his relationship with a number of players.

The two sides worked out their differences and Sharpe played, even catching a key touchdown pass. But the damage had been done.

Sharpe also suffered a severe toe injury early that season, so painful that he couldn't practice the last half of the season.

Over the years he had also suffered rib and knee injuries but played through them, too. But then in a December game against Atlanta, on a seemingly innocuous block, Sharpe collapsed to the ground with numbness in his arms. The next week, he was cleared to play in Tampa but the numbness returned. He was soon diagnosed with a narrowing of his spinal cord, a condition he had been born with.

After surgery, which forced him to miss the entire 1995 season, he tried to return but when the Packers asked him to take a pay cut, he refused and was released.

He remains second on the Packers' all-time receptions list with 595 catches as well as 8,154 yards and 65 touchdowns. He was named to five Pro Bowls and was a three-time All-Pro.

He was inducted into the Packers Hall of Fame in 2002, and there are many around the NFL, including his Hall of Fame brother, Shannon, who believe Sterling belongs in Canton. Shannon even said in his Hall induction that he's only the second-best football player in his family.

None of this concerns Sharpe even today.

Asked in the summer of 2018 by Luke Fox of SportsNet how much football he followed these days, he said none.

And he added this.

"I did what I wanted to do. I wanted to play in the National Football League," he said. "The only thing I ever asked God for was, 'I want to play in the NFL.' I didn't ask to play for 10 years, 15 years, four years. I just wanted to play, and I got a chance. Doesn't get any better than that."

DONALD DRIVER

The NFL has had its fair share of long shots who, given the right opportunity and motivation and a decent amount of luck, have not only found a place in the league, but flourished.

But has there ever been anyone who did more with seemingly less than Donald Driver?

He was the Packers' last pick in the 1999 draft, a seventh-rounder from Alcorn State and the 213th player taken. For context, only 40 other players were drafted after Driver.

Donald Driver in 2011

But the Packers were intrigued by Driver's sheer athleticism, borne of the fact that he was an Olympic-quality high jumper. No one expected him to make the team, but he was one of those luxury picks that cost the Packers nothing.

But a funny thing happened. Driver, who had spent part of his youth homeless in his native Houston, was made of sterner stuff and never viewed himself as someone who didn't belong in the NFL.

And for 14 seasons, he was a reliable and consistent wide receiver who would go from unknown to the Packers' all-time leader in receptions and receiving yards.

"I always knew I could play in this league," he said.

He was never especially flashy and was never considered a deep threat despite his speed. Over his career he averaged just 13.6 yards per reception, but there were times when the explosiveness was on display for all to see.

For example, in the 2008 NFC Championship Game against the New York Giants at a frigid Lambeau Field, Driver gathered in a 90-yard catch and run that stunned the Giants.

In a 2010 game against the San Francisco 49ers, Driver caught a pass and proceeded to break five tackles and elude two others for a 61-yard score.

But mostly he was as consistent as the sunrise, and the Packers grew to appreciate that effort game in and game out.

In a six-season period, from 2004 to 2009, Driver caught at least 70 passes a season and gained more than 1,000 yards. And on October 18, 2009, in a game against the Detroit Lions, Driver surpassed Sterling Sharpe as the Packers' all-time leader in receptions.

Two seasons later, against the Carolina Panthers, he would own the team record for receiving yards as well.

Driver's impact began to fade after 2010 as younger receivers like Jordy Nelson and Greg Jennings began to receive more playing time.

In February 2013 Driver announced his retirement. He left with no regrets and nothing left undone, a testament to all the dreamers who think they don't have a chance to make it at the highest levels of sport.

"I played my entire career in Green Bay and have always enjoyed a special bond with the fans," Driver said in a statement released by the team. "I can think of no better way to retire than to celebrate with them and the Packers organization."

He finished his career with 743 receptions for 10,137 yards and 61 touchdowns. He was a two-time Pro Bowler and was inducted into the Packers Hall of Fame in 2017.

JAMES LOFTON

He was the classic deep threat. The receiver that defensive backs both thrilled in covering and were terrified of trying to cover.

James Lofton came along at the perfect time for an NFL that was moving rapidly toward the aerial circus that would make the game even more popular than it already was.

And the Green Bay Packers, who made Lofton their first-round pick in the 1978 draft, benefited mightily.

It actually all started in the 1978 home opener against the New Orleans Saints when the rookie caught three passes (all for touchdowns) for 107 yards.

For nine seasons the Packers offense revolved around Lofton and his ability to get open, preferably 30 yards downfield.

He missed only one game in that time and caught 530 passes for 9,656 yards, a staggering average of 18 yards per catch. In 1983 and 1984 he also led the league by averaging more than 22 yards per catch.

As many Packers fans know, Lofton did not leave Green Bay on the best of terms as he was traded in April 1987, in the wreckage of Lofton's trial in late 1986 for second-degree sexual assault (for which he was found not guilty).

But the Packers in that period were a mess in many ways, and it became easier to deal him to the Los Angeles Raiders for third- and fourth-round draft picks. Lofton wasn't happy.

Time, however, has eased the hard feelings and Lofton recalls just how special a place Green Bay was to play football.

Lofton would go on to play for the Raiders, Buffalo Bills, Los Angeles Rams, and Philadelphia Eagles in a career that saw him catch a total of 764 passes for 14,004 yards, making him the first player to reach 14,000 yards in receptions.

James Lofton
GREEN BAY PACKERS VIA WIKIMEDIA
COMMONS

After 16 seasons he retired in 1993 without any second thoughts. After all, he said there weren't many spots available on NFL teams for 37-year-old receivers who couldn't out-run defenders any longer.

But he will primarily be remembered for his accomplishments as a Green Bay Packer: seven-time Pro Bowler, a member of the 1978 NFL All-Rookie Team, as well as a part of the 1980s NFL All-Decade Team. He was inducted into the Packers Hall of Fame in 1999 and the Pro Football Hall of Fame in 2003.

JORDY NELSON

The irony, of course, is that in 2009, when the Green Bay Packers drafted a wide receiver from Kansas State named Jordy Nelson, not many Packers fans knew who he was. When he was released prior to the 2018 season, few fans could imagine the Packers without him.

Such is life in the NFL.

If any player was ever made to be a Packer, it was Nelson. A country kid who played the game hard and squeezed every bit of talent out of his body, he made himself into one of the league's best receivers. Even a preseason knee injury that ended his 2015 season before it started could not stop him, and he came back better and stronger than ever.

But it was his release in the spring of 2018 that stunned teammates and fans and left many wondering just what the Packers were up to.

Yes, there was a new young hotshot waiting in the wings, Davante Adams, but Nelson had plenty left and, though his contract was up, he was willing to take a pay cut to remain in Green Bay to keep catching touchdown passes from his close friend Aaron Rodgers.

But it wasn't to be and when Nelson was cut, he made it clear he wasn't happy.

"It hurt," he told ESPN.com. "The thing that bothered me the most was that the Packers didn't seem to want to make it work."

Rodgers was angry, too, though he tried to be somewhat diplomatic.

Jordy Nelson (87) in the huddle, 2012. There's a good chance the ball is coming his way.
MIKE MORBECK VIA WIKIMEDIA COMMONS

"It's not my call," he said. "But I can tell you this, we will miss him."

And the Packers' 6-9-1 record, their second straight losing season, seemed to make that clear.

Nelson immediately signed with the Oakland Raiders, where he went on to have another terrific season.

What remains, though, are the memories of Nelson, who quietly and efficiently piled up 550 receptions, fourth-best in team history, with 7,848 yards (fourth-best) and 69 touchdowns (second-most in history among Packers receivers). And that's with missing an entire season. But in 2016, after undergoing knee surgery, Nelson came back better than ever, catching 97 passes for 1,257 yards and a league-best 14 touchdowns. For his efforts he was named the NFL Comeback Player of the Year.

"Jordy has been a wonderful representative for the Packers and Green Bay," said team president Mark Murphy.

Packers fans still wonder what might have been if Nelson were still with the team. But to many fans, he will always be a Packer, no matter where he plays.

After the 2018 season, and after battling more injuries, Nelson was released by the Raiders. And while there was some interest league-wide in signing the dependable receiver (though not from the Packers), he retired.

In time he will earn his entrance into the Packers Hall of Fame.

AND THE WINNERS ARE . . .

Donald Driver is the Packers' all-time leading receiver and that counts for a lot. But the three receivers on this select, and most unusual, all-star team must reflect skills you can't find just anywhere—especially with a demanding coach like Vince Lombardi and a perfectionist quarterback like Aaron Rodgers.

So the receivers here are **Don Hutson, Sterling Sharpe,** and **James Lofton.** Hutson makes it because of his early and dramatic impact on the NFL and the Packers as a franchise, as well as the fact that with his size and speed there's no reason he couldn't be just as effective in today's NFL. Sharpe brings the rugged possession-receiver aspect to this team. If it's third down and eight yards are needed for a first down, Sharpe is the guy to make that catch. And Lofton brings the always necessary and ever-present long-distance threat. He can score on any play and from anywhere on the field. No matter how you cut it, that's a formidable trio.

WIDE RECEIVERS WHO DID NOT MAKE THE CUT

It is so tempting to include another player from the 2018 roster on this team. But **Davante Adams,** despite posting one of the best seasons in team history during a forgettable '18 campaign, still needs just a little more time. A second-round draft pick in 2014 from Fresno State, Adams not only has emerged as the Packers' top receiver but is one of the best young pass catchers in the league. In 2018 he caught 111 passes for 1,386 yards and 13 touchdowns while he was double- and, in some cases, triple-teamed. Adams could have set team records in both receptions and yardage but a knee injury sidelined him in the season finale. He missed the receiving record held by Sterling Sharpe by just two catches and the yardage record, owned by Jordy Nelson, by 133. In five seasons he has already amassed 348 receptions, ranking him 10th in team history. If he stays healthy, the sky's the limit with Adams.

Antonio Freeman was a third-round draft pick in 1995 who made his first impression his rookie season with a 76-yard punt return for a touchdown in a playoff win over the Atlanta Falcons. He would evolve into a wily, reliable wide receiver who would be a key to the Packers not only reaching Super Bowl XXXI, but winning it. He caught three passes for 195 yards in the win over the Patriots, including an 81-yard catch and run that he still calls his best reception as a Packer. He also caught two touchdown passes in the Super Bowl XXXII loss to Denver, and in 1998 he had his best season—catching 84 passes for a league-best 1,424 yards and 14 touchdowns. In his two stints with the Packers (he spent one intervening season in Philadelphia, in 2002) he caught 431 passes, still seventh-best in team history, and scored 57 touchdowns. He was inducted into the Packers Hall of Fame in 2009.

In his seven seasons with the Packers, **Greg Jennings** always seemed to be involved in something special. As a rookie second-round pick from Western Michigan University in 2006, he caught Brett Favre's 400th touchdown pass, a milestone only one other quarterback (Dan Marino) had reached at that time. The next season, he caught Favre's 420th touchdown pass, tying Favre with Marino for the most TD passes in NFL history. The following week against the Minnesota Vikings, Jennings caught Favre's tie-breaking 421st touchdown pass. Later that season against the Dallas Cowboys, with Favre sidelined due to an injury, Jennings hauled in the first-ever touchdown pass from Aaron Rodgers. Jennings was a versatile, tough receiver who could make the catch in a crowd and get deep for the long ball. And in the biggest games, he always showed up, catching two touchdowns in Green Bay's Super Bowl win over Pittsburgh as well as a critical reception late to keep a drive going.

In 2013 he signed with the Minnesota Vikings, spending two seasons there before going on to the Miami Dolphins. He retired after the 2015 season. He finished his Packers career with 425 receptions for an average of more than 15 yards a catch and scored 53 touchdowns, sixth-best in team history. And all that in just 96 games.

Let's go back, before the Super Bowls and the high-flying offenses that make up the NFL these days. **Billy Howton** was an awfully good receiver in an era when wide receivers were still gaining a foothold in the evolving NFL. He was drafted in 1952 and made a thunderous impact as a rookie, catching 53 passes for 1,231 yards (an NFL rookie record) and 13 touchdowns (also a record) and drawing comparisons among Packers faithful as the next Don Hutson. In seven seasons with the Packers, Howton caught 303 passes and averaged more than 18 yards per catch. He also scored 43 touchdowns. He was a four-time Pro Bowler and was named All-Pro twice. He also led the league twice in receiving yards and yards per game. He was inducted into the Packers Hall of Fame in 1974.

KICKER

The Candidates
Chris Jacke
Ryan Longwell
Mason Crosby

Longtime Packers fans remember all too well something that, through time and legend, should be called "the Season of the Four Kickers." Those who were not around and have only heard tales of that season should probably be glad they did not witness it in person. Those who did witness it? Well, it epitomized just how lost their beloved franchise was back then.

It was 1988 and, in an era where very little went right, this might well have been rock bottom for a franchise that was going nowhere fast.

The Packers had a new coach in Lindy Infante, the guy who took the job after the guy who said he wanted the job, Michigan State University head man George Perles, changed his mind.

It was a franchise that had sputtered badly for years, as fans watched a dynasty collapse, followed by years of uncertainty and mediocrity and preceded by the undisciplined crew who made up the Packers of coach Forrest Gregg.

Infante stepped into a difficult situation and hoped to make things better.

But that didn't happen. In fact, the Packers of 1988 were even worse than the team left behind by Gregg.

What made it even worse for Infante was that with all of the other glaring weaknesses on his team, the one he hadn't given much thought to was his field goal kicker.

Max Zendejas had joined the Packers in 1987 as a replacement kicker during the NFL players strike. He had done a solid job, making all seven of his kicks before the conflict was settled and the "real" players came back.

Zendejas stuck around with the Packers and eventually replaced veteran kicker Al Del Greco, who had missed half his attempts in five games.

In some ways, this was the start of the Packers' extended kicking woes.

Zendejas made 9 of 16 field goals and was brought back for 1988, allowing Infante to work on other things like a disastrous quarterback situation, no running game, and a lousy defense.

And Zendejas seemed to have everything under control, including four field goals in a big win over the Minnesota Vikings.

But the kicking situation, and the Packers' season, unraveled the following week in a rainy Milwaukee County Stadium.

Facing the defending Super Bowl champion Redskins, the Packers hung around gamely and had a chance to tie the game with a mere 24-yard field goal with 11 seconds to play.

But Zendejas, who had previously kicked for the Redskins, missed the kick and sent the Packers to their sixth loss in eight games.

The Redskins were exultant afterward.

"I want to send him a Christmas present!" Redskins defensive end Dexter Manley said in a story by the *Washington Post*. "Believe me, I knew Max Zendejas wouldn't let us down—he's a true Redskin."

Afterward, Zendejas had no excuses.

"I just wanted to make the kick," he said sadly.

But he didn't, and in the NFL failure is not an option. Zendejas had also missed two extra points, and for a team already struggling to score points, changes were needed.

So over the course of the final eight weeks of an interminable season (the loss to Washington was the first in a seven-game losing streak), three more kickers would take a crack at doing a job that, at least in Green Bay, seemed more difficult than splitting an atom.

Dale Dawson got the first shot. He made three of five field goals and only one of two extra points in four games. Of course, it helped Dawson that the Packers were shut out in his first two games.

Exit Dawson and enter Dean Dorsey, who made an inauspicious debut by missing two field goals in a 16–0 loss to the Chicago Bears. He lasted three games, making one of three kicks and missing an extra point in a win over the Vikings.

In the season finale, the Packers took a look at Curtis Burrow, who was truly terrible. He missed his only field goal attempt and two of four extra points, leading many to wonder if it was legal in the NFL Collective Bargaining Agreement for the Packers to release him during the game.

That season four kickers made just 13 of 25 field goals and, worse yet, only 23 of 29 extra points. The 4-12 slog was over and Infante knew he needed to address the kicking situation. He drafted Chris Jacke out of the University of Texas–El Paso, and since then the Packers' kicking has been stable.

As 1988 proved, it's no walk in the park being the place-kicker. Kicking in Green Bay is tougher than kicking anywhere else in the NFL because not only does the tradition of kicking in Lambeau Field have its own set of mental roadblocks, but often the weather can be just nasty enough to make an already difficult job even tougher.

Some kickers thrive and some don't.

And as the list above shows, there are hardy, tough souls who can handle the job physically and mentally and still make a difficult job look almost routine.

Almost.

In fact, our list of all-star finalists are the three kickers who have made Green Bay their place of business since 1989, save for one season.

Chris Jacke kicked eight seasons for the Packers. Ryan Longwell kicked another nine. Mason Crosby has handled the job since 2007. The only aberration? That was in 2006 when Dave Rayner handled the chores and did it well, making 26 of 35 field goals.

But it's been the trio of Jacke, Longwell, and Crosby who have seen it all in their combined 29 seasons (through the 2018 season).

They have seen it all, from last-second kicks that have won games to those agonizing misses that spelled eventual defeat. They have been heroes and they have been vilified, but they all know that next week, there's a chance to do it all over again.

CHRIS JACKE

Boy, did the Packers need this guy. Normally drafting a kicker is a luxury for teams, but the Packers were desperate and in the sixth round of the 1989 draft, they selected Jacke.

Ironically, this was the infamous Packers draft when they bypassed the likes of running back Barry Sanders, linebacker Derrick Thomas, and cornerback Deion Sanders to select tackle Tony Mandarich, who still earns a spot as one of the great busts in NFL history.

Obviously, it was not a great draft for Green Bay as, of the 14 players selected, only defensive tackle Matt Brock and running back Vince Workman provided much for any length of service.

But Jacke was the right choice at the right time and, despite knowing the team's pathetic recent history, he was anxious for the challenge.

Even so, the Packers brought numerous free agent kickers into training camp because, as they had learned painfully the year before, there was no such thing as being too careful.

But Jacke exuded a confidence that pleased the coaching staff.

He knew he was the right kicker at the right time and all he needed was a chance to prove himself.

And he did. In a 1989 season that was one for the ages, the Packers rebounded with 10 wins, with seven of those wins decided by four points or fewer. Jacke himself played with the savvy of a veteran, kicking three game-winning field goals.

"That season was a lot of fun," he recalled. "It seemed like it was something new every week."

He made 22 of 28 field goals and quickly entrenched himself as a key member of the Packers' resurgence—which would begin in 1992 with the arrival of general manager Ron Wolf and head coach Mike Holmgren.

They changed the direction and the culture and, after years of mediocrity, the Packers began winning.

Jacke went on to kick for eight seasons in Green Bay, making 77 percent of his kicks and scoring 820 points, then a record for Packers kickers and second only to the peerless Hall of Famer Don Hutson in terms of total points.

But Jacke always marched to his own drummer, and his eccentric ways started to rub the organization (read: Holmgren) the wrong way. And when he missed a team Super Bowl ring presentation prior to the start of the 1997 season, the Packers had reached their limit.

By the same token, Jacke was angered when the Packers drafted another kicker, Penn State's Brett Conway, that April. Jacke saw it as a direct challenge to his performance and believed that they had lost faith in him.

Already a free agent, he decided it was time to move on and signed with the Pittsburgh Steelers. He never played for Pittsburgh due to a chronic hip injury, but he did sign later with the Washington Redskins and the following year with the Arizona Cardinals, where he kicked for two seasons before retiring.

He has remained in the Green Bay area and runs a players' speakers bureau called Player Alumni Resources. In 2013 he was inducted into the Packers Hall of Fame, and he still keeps track of the team he remains close to.

RYAN LONGWELL

He was called a "camp leg," and Ryan Longwell was OK with that.

Ryan Longwell prepares to kick in 2004.
WIKIMEDIA COMMONS

In the summer of 1997, he was signed as a free agent by the defending Super Bowl champion Packers. He had kicked well for the University of California and decided to sign with the Packers to give the team's newest kicker, Brett Conway, something to think about.

After all, Conway was the future of the Packers kicking game. The Packers, perhaps with a touch of arrogance, selected Conway (a four-year star at Penn State) in the third round of the draft and expected him to slip seamlessly into the role Jacke had held for so long.

Longwell? He was brought in as an insurance policy. He would kick in practice, maybe a preseason game or two, and perhaps catch the eye of other NFL teams in need of a kicker.

But, once again, the vagaries of the NFL came into play.

Conway missed his first four kicks in the preseason, showed a surprising lack of distance in training camp, and generally showed very little to a shocked coaching staff. To make matters worse, during pregame warmups prior to a preseason game in Oakland, Conway severely pulled a thigh muscle in his right leg and was sidelined.

Longwell stepped in, and on his first attempt as a pro kicker shanked a 26-yard field goal. But the Raiders were called for offsides and Longwell got another shot, this time drilling a 21-yard kick. He'd make two more field goals that game and, suddenly, there was a potential kicker controversy.

But that never developed, as Longwell continued to kick well and Conway's injury never healed. The highly touted draft pick was placed on injured reserve and the job belonged to Longwell. He would end up being superb.

With the bright lights of the regular season on in a Monday night season opener against the Chicago Bears, Longwell made all three of his field goal attempts, and he was off and running.

Almost.

As any NFL kicker can explain in all too painful detail, a series of triumphs can be undone by a single mistake. There is little room for failure, and kickers have been known to win a game one week with a clutch kick and lose their job the next by bad weather or bad luck or bad kicks.

After his superb opener against the Bears, Longwell took his game on the road for the first time as the Packers played the Philadelphia Eagles. It was a struggle all afternoon for the Packers at rugged Veterans Stadium. But Longwell seemed oblivious to the pressure, kicking three field goals to keep the Packers in the game against the hapless Eagles.

Trailing 10–9, the Packers put together a late drive, moving to the Eagles' 12. Onto the field trotted Longwell to kick what seemed to be a simple 29-yard field goal to win the game.

However, as Longwell ran out, the skies opened up and rain poured down on the stadium's artificial turf. It lasted for only a minute or so, but it was just long enough to made the field slick. So as Longwell stepped into the kick, his left foot slipped and the ball sailed wide.

It is a kicker's worst nightmare, but afterward Longwell faced the media barrage calmly and answered all the questions posed to him about how and why he missed the kick. Asked if he thought the Packers might make a change at kicker, he simply smiled.

"I guess they could," he said.

But they didn't. Longwell went on to make 24 of his 30 field goals that season, and the guy who wasn't supposed to stay around past August kicked for the Packers in Super Bowl XXXII in January 1998.

As for Conway, he was released and bounced around the league through the 2003 season, kicking at various times for the Washington Redskins, New York Giants, Oakland Raiders, New York Jets, and Cleveland Browns, playing a total of 51 games.

Longwell spent nine seasons with the Packers, making 82 percent of his field goals, and at one time holding the spot as the Packers' all-time leading scorer with 1,054 points (226 field goals, 376 extra points). He's now fallen to second behind Mason Crosby.

And though Longwell became entrenched in the Green Bay community during his near decade with the Packers, when free agency loomed in 2006, the Minnesota Vikings made an offer Longwell couldn't refuse. So he signed with the Packers' division rival, where he was even better, making 86 percent of his kicks in six seasons.

He was released after the 2011 season and latched on briefly with the Seattle Seahawks before retiring.

In 2018 Longwell was inducted into the Packers Hall of Fame. And perhaps no one was more appreciative to be inducted than Longwell, who cherished every moment of every game.

"It's a dream come true that never really was part of the dream," he told Packers.com prior to the ceremony. "I was trying to get from one week to the next week."

He did a whole lot better than that.

MASON CROSBY

It was not just a bad season for Mason Crosby. It was a season that, according to all the unspoken and unwritten laws of the NFL, should have sent him to the sidewalk.

In 2012, Crosby, the Packers' sixth-round draft choice in 2007 who had put in five solid if not quite spectacular seasons, had lost his ability to make the kicks he needed to make.

That season was one that keeps all kickers awake at night. In 16 games Crosby made 21 of 33 field goals, a disastrous 64 percent. It was the worst performance by a full-time Packers kicker since the dreaded days of 1988 when Max Zendejas made just 56 percent of his kicks. He didn't last—Crosby did.

Still, it got so bad for Crosby and the Packers that season that head coach Mike McCarthy eventually stopped calling on Crosby to attempt field goals, instead going on fourth down to try to score or gain a first down. He also missed field goals in eight straight games, an almost unheard-of event in these days of the modern field goal kicker.

Mason Crosby attempts a field goal against Washington, 2018.
KEITH ALLISON VIA WIKIMEDIA COMMONS

There were full-throated calls from Packers fans to replace Crosby with someone, anyone, and Crosby admitted years later he wasn't so sure they weren't right.

"It was looking a little dire in the middle of that one," Crosby told the *Milwaukee Journal Sentinel.*

But a strange thing happened. The Packers did not do what every other team in the league would have done. They did not jettison the kicker who had performed so well for them in the previous seasons. They chalked it up to technical issues in his approach as well as human nature—the worse he got, the more he pressed and the worse it continued to be.

Yet the Packers didn't just pretend not to notice either. Prior to the 2013 season, they cut his salary and restructured it to be more incentive-based. If he kicked the way the team knew he could, he'd be rewarded.

All Crosby did was respond with the best season of his career, hitting 33 of 37 kicks.

He remained grateful to the Packers for continuing to show faith in him and in 2015, when he kicked his fourth field goal of the game against Seattle, Crosby passed Ryan Longwell as the Packers' all-time scoring leader.

And the 2012 season to forget? He forgot it.

"I've come out of that and feel like my best years obviously have been these last few, and I feel like my best years are ahead of me," he told the *Journal Sentinel.* "I'm really happy with that and how I handled my business and my approach."

Though Crosby has kicked for the Packers through the 2018 season, nothing is taken for granted or expected. Indeed, in a 2018 game against the Detroit Lions, Crosby missed four of five field goal attempts and an extra point, rekindling thoughts of the bad old days six years earlier. But in typical fashion, Crosby responded by making nine of his next 10 kicks.

Success followed by failure and back again—such is the life of a field goal kicker.

And the Winner Is . . .

The NFL has evolved in so many ways over the years that what was important five years ago may not even register on the radar any longer. But this has not changed: field goal kickers must be accurate and consistent. After all, this is a league where points are too precious and too hard won, whether it's a touchdown or a field goal. The three kickers we have nominated have shown through long, hard, and often trying times that they have what it takes to make kicks when necessary. Any of these three could do the job, and did the job, when called upon.

But the edge here goes to the most consistent guy, and that's **Ryan Longwell**. In his nine seasons with the Packers, he connected on 82 percent of his field goals, and that included an uncharacteristic 2001 season when he made only 65 percent of his kicks. Every other year, he was as constant as the sunrise.

Jacke made 77 percent of his field goals but was never considered a sure thing, and Crosby, though impressive in his rally from a disastrous 2012 season, has always been prone to bad misses at the worst time.

Kickers Who Did Not Make the Cut

Chester Marcol was different—even for a kicker. His thick, black-framed glasses poked out from the single bar on his facemask and his diminutive stature resembled that of a CPA instead of a professional football player. But looks were deceiving, because the little guy from Opole, Poland, could kick.

Indeed, in his nine seasons with the Packers, there were times he was most of the offense since the Packers of the early '70s had trouble finding the end zone. He was the NFL Rookie of the Year in 1972 with his 33 field goals as well as a two-time All-Pro. His 521 points is seventh all-time in team history. He was inducted into the Packers Hall of Fame in 1987.

Jan Stenerud spent only a little more than three seasons with the Packers (1980–83) but still made an impact. He had already put together a Hall of Fame career after 13 seasons with the Kansas City Chiefs, where he departed as the team's all-time leading scorer. But when he was released late in the 1980 season, the Packers were desperate for a quality kicker given that both Chester Marcol and Tom Birney had sputtered. Stenerud signed on for the final four games of the season, made three of five kicks, and went on to become Green Bay's kicker through the 1983 season, hitting 59 of 73 field goals. But coach Bart Starr was fired after the '83 season and new coach Forrest Gregg decided to move on from the veteran Stenerud. He went on to kick for the Minnesota Vikings (and earn a Pro Bowl berth) while the Packers once again struggled over the next five years to find a reliable kicker. Stenerud was inducted into both the Packers Hall of Fame and the Pro Football Hall of Fame in 1991.

Fred Cone had his moments, too. He played for some awful Packers teams in the 1950s and points were at a premium. As well, kicking field goals in that era was much more of an adventure than it is now. He kicked for Green Bay for seven seasons (1951–57) and led the league in field goals with 16 in 1955. His 455 points is eighth in team history. He was inducted into the Packers Hall of Fame in 1974.

KICK RETURNER

The Only Candidate
Desmond Howard

Our final offensive position may well be going the way of the dinosaur. In today's NFL, the kickoff and, to a lesser extent, the punt return are the subject of great debate among league officials who see those two often exciting but always dangerous events as the reason for many of the injuries, sometimes catastrophic, incurred by players.

And they're not wrong.

Pro football in its first five decades featured, for the most part, players of relatively the same size. Defensive linemen, for example, were 240 pounds and speed, while always valued by coaches, was usually the province of wide receivers and running backs.

But over the past few decades, the players, having trained since they were kids, are now much bigger, much stronger, and much faster at all positions.

And statistics show that fully half of football injuries (from high school to the NFL) occur when large, fast, angry guys fly at full speed into equally large, fast, angry guys who are trying to stop them from crushing the ball carrier. The collisions are often epic.

Rule changes have taken some of the sting out of kickoffs and punts, and while returning kicks remains a dangerous job, most of the time the new rules result in touchbacks and fair catches.

But on those rare occasions when a kick returner finds a seam or a punt returner breaks a tackle? Oh, my. It remains one of the most scintillating plays in all of sports. And, more often than not, it can change the course of a game.

We will resist providing multiple candidates for the Packers all-time all-star team at this position because, in truth, there is only one player who merits consideration.

He spent only one full season in Green Bay and nearly didn't make it out of training camp. But Desmond Howard was the epitome of being in the right place at the right time and, without his record-setting 1996 season, the Packers may not have won Super Bowl XXXI. He was a game-changer in every sense of the word, and his biggest mistake was deciding to grab the big money of free agency and leave a team that was built for long-term greatness.

Howard came into the NFL with impeccable credentials. The University of Michigan wide receiver and kick returner won just about every college award there was to win in 1991, including the Heisman Trophy.

In the 1992 NFL Draft, the defending Super Bowl champion Washington Redskins traded several draft picks to move up to the fourth spot and selected Howard, whom they saw as a complement to their already strong receiving corps and a bridge to the future.

"He doesn't have any flaws," Redskins coach Joe Gibbs said at the time. "We're excited."

But it became clear fairly quickly that he did have flaws—including poor route running and a tendency to drop passes. Plus his size, at 5-foot-10 and 180 pounds, went against the league trend for taller and stronger wide receivers.

Howard spent three seasons with the Redskins and caught just 66 passes. He also didn't set the NFL on fire with his return abilities, so in 1995 the Redskins left Howard unprotected in the expansion draft and he was taken by the new Jacksonville Jaguars.

He didn't do much there either and, after one season, he signed as a free agent with the Packers.

After four seasons, the talk was that Howard was another spectacular Heisman Trophy– winning flameout and if he didn't make it with the up-and-coming powerhouse in Green Bay, his career could well be over.

And Howard seemed ready to be sent packing from Green Bay as well, as a nagging hip injury kept him from showing the coaching staff anything.

But a terrific preseason performance against the Pittsburgh Steelers that included a punt return for a touchdown secured a roster spot for Howard.

He took it from there.

In the third game of the season, Howard returned a punt 65 yards for a score in a rout of the San Diego Chargers. After that he became a force for an already dangerous Packers team.

He ended up leading the NFL in punt returns (58), punt return yardage (875), and average yards per return (15.1 yards). He also returned three punts for touchdowns.

And he continued his remarkable performance in the playoffs.

In a driving, freezing rainstorm at Lambeau Field, Howard returned a punt 71 yards for the opening touchdown against the San Francisco 49ers, who had made it public all week they would not let Howard beat them. He then returned the next punt 46 yards to set up Green Bay's second touchdown as the Packers rolled, 35–14.

In the NFC title game win over the Carolina Panthers, this time on a frozen Lambeau Field, he averaged 26 yards on kick-off returns, returning one 46 yards.

"We were beginning to think that every time he touched the ball he'd score," said Packers safety LeRoy Butler.

Then he saved his best for last. In Super Bowl XXXI against the New England Patriots, who also insisted the kick returner would not be allowed to beat them, he did just that.

After cutting Green Bay's lead to 27–21 midway through the third quarter, the Patriots kicked to Howard, who brought the ball straight back upfield, breaking two tackles and running 99 yards for the decisive touchdown.

"We had the momentum and he took it away from us," Patriots coach Bill Parcells bemoaned afterward.

For the game, Howard's combined kickoff and punt return yardage of 244 yards tied a Super Bowl record and earned him MVP honors—the first and, so far, only time a special teams player has won the award.

Not surprisingly, Howard was hailed as a hero among Packers fans, and he made a point of thanking the Packers organization often for not losing faith in him during his troubled preseason.

But he had signed only a one-year deal with the Packers, and when the Oakland Raiders came calling with a massive deal, he left the team that had given him what many thought was his last chance.

He never duplicated his magical 1996 season, and in 1999 he actually returned to the Packers. But you can't repeat the past, and at midseason he was traded to Detroit, where he had some success. He retired after the 2002 season.

Does one season make a career? In most cases the answer is no. But for one incredible season, Howard was perhaps the most dangerous player in the NFL and every time a kick landed in his arms, no one knew what might happen. For that reason, and for that season alone, our all-star kick returner is **Desmond Howard**.

Returners Who Did Not Make the Cut

There have been other kick returners who have flashed briefly only to fade away. **Allen Rossum** was traded by the Eagles to the Packers in 2000 and had some nice success, averaging 10 yards per punt return in 2001, returning one kickoff for a touchdown in 2000, and bringing a punt back for a score in 2001. The Packers were impressed with Rossum, and when he became a free agent after the '01 season, they promised to match any offer he might receive. The Atlanta Falcons did indeed make an offer, but that offer never reached the Packers and Rossum joined the Falcons, where in five years he became the team's all-time leader in kickoff and punt return yardage.

From 2013 to 2016, cornerback **Micah Hyde** was Green Bay's primary kick returner and his average was pretty impressive. He averaged 9.7 yards per punt return and 24 yards per kickoff return. He also scored three touchdowns on punt returns—one in 2013 and two in 2014.

DEFENSE

DEFENSIVE ENDS

The Candidates
Reggie White
Willie Davis
Kabeer Gbaja-Biamila

If there is a rock-star position on the defense, look no further than end. It is the position every team covets. Every year, the goal is to find a fast, quick, physical, intelligent player who can either blow past a rival tackle or simply overwhelm him and get to the quarterback. The edge rusher, as he's come to be known, is the player who can unsettle the quarterback and, thus, unsettle the opponent.

Every Packers fan knows how the fortunes of their team changed when Reggie White signed. He instantly made the Packers a force with just the mere thought that he might get to the quarterback.

Green Bay has had its share of quality ends going back to the Lombardi years, and nothing has changed in today's NFL. A pass-rusher is paramount, and the Packers have known some of the best.

REGGIE WHITE

Before the quarterback sack statistic became part of the pro football lexicon in 1982, defensive ends labored in relative anonymity, content to know that what they accomplished mattered to themselves, their teammates, and, yes, the quarterbacks who were on the business end of that mayhem.

But once the stat began to be kept (in fact, it wasn't until 1961 that the NFL even began keeping track of yardage lost by quarterbacks) and the description of it as a "sack" took root, defensive ends became the rock stars of the defense.

Sure, linebackers and tackles and even defensive backs could get in on the sack attack. But it was the defensive ends, with their speed and agility and their belief there was no offensive lineman who could stop them, who benefited most.

And for 15 years, no one was better at destroying quarterbacks than Reggie White.

He developed his reputation at the University of Tennessee. He was a new breed of pass rusher who combined size and speed and technique with a quickness no one had ever seen from a player that size before. If he didn't plow over an offensive tackle with his brute force, he would blow past him with his speed. And when he got a quarterback in his grasp, he never let him go.

Naturally, NFL teams were drooling over the possibility of eventually landing him.

But it didn't quite work out that way. While the NFL waited anxiously, White shocked everyone in 1984 by signing to play with the Memphis Showboats of the rival United States Football League. White said the opportunity to play pro football in his home state (he grew up in Chattanooga) was the determining factor. And in two seasons with the Showboats,

White racked up 23½ sacks in 36 games, while also recovering one fumble for a touchdown and recording a safety.

But the USFL collapsed after the 1985 season and White signed a four-year, $1.85 million contract with the Philadelphia Eagles in which the Eagles also bought out the remaining three years of his Showboats contract.

His impact was immediate and dramatic.

Though joining the Eagles three games into their season, he still amassed 13 sacks and would go on to become the dominant pass rusher in the NFL.

In his eight seasons with the Eagles, and over the course of 121 games, he accumulated 124 sacks, including a then record 21 sacks in one season, in 1987.

White redefined the role of the defensive end and he led an Eagles defense that was among the best and most fearsome.

Indeed, in the five seasons from 1988 to 1992, the Eagles rode that defense to the playoffs four times and posted a 52-28 record.

Yet once the playoffs arrived, the Eagles stumbled, not even reaching the NFC Championship Game. That failure began to wear on White, whose sole goal was to reach a Super Bowl and win it.

The rumblings of White's unhappiness began in the 1992 season as he saw Philly's title window closing. He knew if he was to reach the only goal that mattered to him, he might have to do it somewhere else.

Then, in a November 1992 game against an upstart Packers team at Milwaukee County Stadium, White took notice of the Packers' young, cocky quarterback, who kept getting up and complimenting White every time White knocked him to the ground.

Indeed, one White hit on Favre actually injured Favre's shoulder. But the quarterback kept playing, completing 23 of 33 passes for 275 yards with two touchdowns as Green Bay posted the 27–24 upset.

"I remember thinking that I could play with this kid," White said.

That off-season, as the Eagles again flamed out in the play-offs, White was ready to exercise his rights as a free agent.

He didn't really want to leave Philadelphia, but he didn't see the Eagles making the personnel moves that would lead to a Super Bowl.

So he began a tour of the NFL to see which teams could prove they were forces not only on the field but also financially.

That spring White visited a number of teams, but it appeared the finalists would be two of the NFL's royalty—the Washington Redskins and San Francisco 49ers.

But suddenly a new team was mentioned, and it brought a combination of snickers and grunts of dismissal. The Green Bay Packers, who for so long had been on the outside looking in, were making a bid. Sure, they had a new coach and an impressive young quarterback and they posted a 9-7 record in '92 that showed, perhaps, that they were on the way up.

But Reggie White in Green Bay? Never.

Yet Packers general manager Ron Wolf knew what other teams did not. They had the cash reserves to front-load a tremendous contract that even the 49ers, who appeared to be the favorite to sign White, couldn't match.

So on April 6, 1993, everything changed—not only for the Packers franchise but for the NFL. White, the top free agent available, signed a four-year, $17 million contact with the Packers.

Bob Harlan, the Packers president who a little more than a year earlier had given Wolf all the power he needed to make the Packers better, recalls that day.

"I remember Reggie said to Mike Holmgren, 'This makes your team better, doesn't it?'" Harlan recalled to the *Milwaukee Journal Sentinel*. "He said, 'Yes, it sure does.'"

More important, White's signing changed the impression of players about playing in Green Bay. If Reggie White would play there, why wouldn't anyone else?

One of those players who signed as a free agent with the Packers in 1995, tight end Keith Jackson, summed it up best in an interview with the *Journal Sentinel*.

"Before that decision guys would say, 'If Green Bay drafts me, I don't want to go.' It was Siberia," said Jackson. "But Reggie White saw something different about it. Reggie saw all these positives about Green Bay that nobody really knew about. He saw it as an opportunity to go somewhere where the people are super fans. And when you lose a game, there's nobody screaming at you saying you're a bum. The media is reporting the facts and not trying to create a controversy. It was actually an oasis to play football, and you really concentrated on being a football player."

And since then, Green Bay has become a go-to spot for players. The days of a draft pick choosing to play in Canada instead of Green Bay (Bruce Clark, come on down) were long gone.

White, an ordained minister, often said it was God who directed him to Green Bay and, of course, there were the cynics who believed there were 17 million reasons he went to Green Bay.

But, whatever the reason, there was more to White than his simply signing on the dotted line in Green Bay. He also delivered on the field.

In his first season, he posted 13 sacks as the Packers reached the playoffs for the first time since 1982. From there the Packers' climb was steady and relentless.

In fact, in all six seasons White was a Packer, they did not miss the playoffs—reaching three NFC Championship Games and two Super Bowls.

White finally reached the pinnacle in the 1996 season, as the Packers roared into Super Bowl XXXI and beat the New England Patriots.

For White, it was the culmination of everything he had worked for, and what made it even better was he got the opportunity to show to everyone watching what he did best.

On back-to-back plays late in the game, White bull-rushed Patriots left tackle Max Lane, knocking him over once, as he posted consecutive sacks on Patriots quarterback Drew Bledsoe. Years later Lane recalled just how relentless and overpowering White was.

After the game, the image burned in the memory of many Packers fans was of White sprinting the length of the field at the crowded Superdome, holding the Lombardi Trophy over his head in pure joy.

That would indeed be the apex of White's career. The Packers returned to the Super Bowl the next season, but he was a nonfactor and the Packers were upset by the Denver Broncos.

In 1998 he posted 16 sacks, his highest total ever with the Packers, and at age 37 was named the NFL's Defensive Player of the Year. But Green Bay fell in the first round of the playoffs to the 49ers.

Mike Holmgren departed as head coach after that season, as did beloved defensive coordinator Fritz Shurmur, who joined Holmgren in Seattle.

And for White, it was time also. He retired as the Packers' all-time sack leader with 68½ as well as the NFL's all-time leader with 192½. After a year away, he returned in 2000 to play for the Carolina Panthers but again retired after one season.

He finished with 198 career sacks, the best in NFL history at the time, but in the intervening years he has lost both titles.

But make no mistake—Reggie White changed the way the position was played, changed the way offenses had to deal with pure pass rushers, and changed the Packer franchise forever.

After his retirement in 2001, White returned to his calling as a minister. His views on religion undoubtedly caused a stir with many people, but few questioned his ardor. He had since grown interested in Judaism and made several trips to Israel to learn more about it.

On December 26, 2004, White died suddenly of a heart attack at age 43. In honor of his career, the Pro Football Hall of Fame waived its requirement that a player must be retired five years before induction into the Hall. In February 2006 White was a first-ballot selection, and that August he took his place in the Hall of Fame.

WILLIE DAVIS

His career was over. Well, maybe not over but at least going nowhere in a hurry. It was 1960 and Willie Davis wasn't sure what awaited him.

A 17th-round draft pick of the Cleveland Browns in 1956, he had already put his career on hold for two years as he fulfilled his military service obligation.

Willie Davis (87) with Henry Jordan on the Packer sidelines
AP PHOTO/VERNON BIEVER

He returned to the Browns in 1958, but in that time the Browns still had not figured out where to play Davis. He had size and agility so he was put on the offensive line and then tried at linebacker, but neither seemed the right fit.

So, almost in a gesture of running up the white flag of surrender, prior to the 1960 season the Browns dealt Davis to the Green Bay Packers for a receiver named A. D. Williams.

Davis wasn't sure what to expect or what to do. His career had sputtered in Cleveland and now he was dealt to Green Bay, a franchise that had done nothing for years. He briefly considered retiring before he talked to the coach who had taken over the Packers the year before.

That coach, Vince Lombardi, saw Davis as another critical piece in putting together a championship team. And unlike in Cleveland, Lombardi knew exactly where to play Davis—defensive end.

"I consider speed, agility, and size to be the three most important attributes for a defensive lineman," Lombardi told Davis at the time. "Give me a man who has any two of those dimensions and he'll do OK. But give me all three and he'll be great. We think you have all three."

It was exactly what Davis needed to hear, and for the next decade he was a force for the Packers defense and took his place as one of the best defensive ends in NFL history.

"Coming to Green Bay was the best thing that ever happened to me," he said.

From 1960 to 1967 he anchored a defense that played in six NFL Championship Games and won five of them, including the first two NFL-AFL Championship Games, known as Super Bowls I and II.

And along the way, Davis was a seemingly permanent fixture, an iron man who played through injury and never missed a game in his 10 seasons with the Packers.

The only things missing from his remarkable resume are the accolades for the numbers he piled up but for which there are no official records.

Davis played in an era when neither tackles nor quarterback sacks were official NFL statistics. But the Professional Football Researchers Association went back in time to look at those numbers generated by the early stars of the NFL and, according to its research, Davis recorded well over 100 quarterback sacks.

Said John Tunney of the PFRA, "It was possibly more than 120," which included a minimum of 40 from the 1963–65 seasons.

If those numbers are correct, Davis is easily the Packers' all-time sack leader. And Davis believes they are correct.

"I would think I would have to be the team's all-time sacks leader," he was quoted by the *Milwaukee Journal Sentinel* as saying. "I played 10 years and I averaged in the teens in sacks for those 10 years. I know I had 25 one season."

But the individual numbers always mattered less to Davis than the team accomplishments—which were extensive.

His first season saw Green Bay reach the NFL title game against the Philadelphia Eagles, the Packers' first appearance in a championship game since their last title in 1944.

The Packers lost that game, but Lombardi's message afterward resonated with Davis.

Sure enough, the Packers were right back in the championship the next season, playing in below-freezing temperatures at City Stadium and blowing out the New York Giants, 37–0.

Davis recalls this being one of his best games, remembering how his former teammate, Hall of Fame tackle Forrest Gregg, said, "I remember your name being called an awful lot [by the public address announcer]."

"That was a game built around confidence," Davis said years later. "It was strictly an attitude. I said, 'I'm not going to be denied today.'"

He also remembers how much fun that game was and how every aspect of the Packers team came together to play something approaching a perfect game.

And so it was for Davis during his entire Packers career. Championships followed in 1962, 1965, 1966, and 1967 as the Packers established themselves as the best team in football.

That last championship, when the Packers beat the Oakland Raiders in Super Bowl II, was almost an afterthought since two weeks earlier the Packers had survived the epic "Ice Bowl" victory over the Dallas Cowboys.

But the veterans knew that an era was coming to an end. Lombardi stepped down as head coach after that season, staying on for one miserable, unfulfilling year as general manager before leaving altogether to take over as head coach and GM in Washington.

Other mainstays like guard Fuzzy Thurston and wideout Max McGee retired, while others like guard Jerry Kramer, linebacker Ray Nitschke, Gregg, and Davis saw it was nearly time to step away, too. Davis played through the 1969 season and retired.

But unlike so many players of that era (not to mention players today), Davis had a life outside football waiting for him.

He had majored in industrial arts at Grambling State University and late in his career with the Packers, he went back to school and earned his master's degree in business from the University of Chicago.

From there he went on to become a successful businessman, working for the Schlitz Brewing Company in Southern California, serving on numerous boards of directors, and becoming president of All Pro Broadcasting, a chain of radio stations in Milwaukee and Los Angeles.

He left football as a five-time Pro Bowler and All-Pro, and he was inducted into the Pro Football Hall of Fame in 1981 and the Packers Hall of Fame in 1975. He still holds the team record for recovered fumbles with 21 and, of course, the number of quarterback sacks will always be an open question.

He has remained an ardent backer of the Packers and, even today, is appreciative of the stroke of good fortune that landed him in Wisconsin. And he realizes being traded to Green Bay constituted the greatest years of his life.

KABEER GBAJA-BIAMILA

His full name is Muhammed-Kabeer Olanrewaju Gbaja-Biamila, but as he became a surprising and fearsome pass rusher for the Packers, everyone knew him as KGB.

He came from nowhere, a fifth-round draft pick in 2000 out of San Diego State University. Expectations were what you'd expect for a guy taken in the middle to late rounds of a draft.

The Packers were certainly intrigued by his size—6-foot-4 and 245 pounds—and physical skills (he was a track star in college and San Diego State's all-time sack leader). But would those skills translate to the NFL, a league littered with players who had the tools to succeed but never did?

It became obvious pretty quickly that this kid was different. Intelligent and curious, he always wanted to know what was happening, why it was happening, and what he could do to contribute.

Gbaja-Biamila grew up in Los Angeles, the son of Nigerian immigrants, and he admitted that the football history of a Wisconsin team was not high on his list of things to learn.

But he learned quickly about the Packers, their history, and the fans who made the place something truly special.

In fact, former team president Bob Harlan gave KGB a guided tour and a history lesson in his first weeks with the team. He explained the team's unique history, which includes a board

Kabeer Gbaja-Biamila (R) and Cullen Jenkins, 2007

of directors, no single owner, the opportunity for fans to buy stock in the team, and the provision that if the franchise ever folds, all proceeds will go to the Green Bay Packers Foundation, and then the Green Bay Packers will simply cease to exist.

He appreciated the time Harlan spent with him and for years after, Gbaja-Biamila made a point of going up to Harlan's office to say hello.

He may not have been cut from the same mold as many NFL players in terms of personality, but on the field he was every bit the player the Packers had hoped he'd be.

Over a four-year span, from 2001 to 2004, he posted double-digit sacks, the only time a Packers player has done that. In that stretch he accumulated 49 sacks with a combination of strength, guile, speed, and a devastating first step that often gave him the advantage on the rival offensive tackle.

It also helped that KGB was used almost exclusively on passing downs.

It was in October 2007 that Gbaja-Biamila broke the Packers' official record for career quarterback sacks with 69, topping the mark set by Reggie White (KGB has since been passed by linebacker Clay Matthews). He would go on to register 74½ sacks before he was released by the Packers late in the 2008 season.

He retired after that and has remained in the Green Bay area, working in charitable foundations.

He earned one Pro Bowl spot in 2003, was the NFL sacks leader in 2004 with 13½, and was inducted into the Packers Hall of Fame in 2013.

AND THE WINNERS ARE . . .

Any of these three would provide headaches for rival offensive linemen. But since we have only two spots, they have to go to the two best ends this franchise has ever seen—**Reggie White** and **Willie Davis**. Perhaps Kabeer Gbaja-Biamila could provide either with a breather without any appreciable drop-off.

But White and Davis were peerless. They were every-down players who were underrated in their defense of the run and almost unstoppable in going after the quarterback.

In the final analysis, if this team needed a fourth-down stop, letting Davis and White loose on a quarterback was always a good bet.

DEFENSIVE ENDS WHO DID NOT MAKE THE CUT

Aaron Kampman was a fifth-round draft pick of the Packers in 2002 out of the University of Iowa and for eight seasons provided steady play from the defensive end spot. He posted 54 sacks and 458 total tackles, forced 12 fumbles, and was named to two Pro Bowls. A fan favorite because of his Midwest roots (an Iowa native), he maintained strong ties with the Packers over the years. He finished his career with the Jacksonville Jaguars.

Another player who got his start in the era when sacks were not an official statistic, **Ezra Johnson**, no doubt had more than the 41½ career sacks he was officially credited with in his 11 seasons in Green Bay. As we learned earlier, quarterback sacks weren't an official NFL statistic until 1982. But by that stage, Johnson was already known as a fearsome pass rusher. A first-round pick in 1977 from tiny Morris Brown College, Johnson finished second, unofficially, in 1978, behind Detroit's Al Baker with 20½ sacks. In 1983 he earned an official season sack title with 14½, the same season the Packers offense was among the most explosive in the NFL while the defense was historically awful. Johnson was also known by many Packers fans for his unfortunate decision in a 1980 preseason game to eat a hot dog on the sidelines. Head coach Bart Starr fined him $1,000, though he gave it back to Johnson at the end of the season. But defensive line coach Fred van Appen was furious that Starr did not suspend Johnson. Five days after the incident, van Appen resigned. Johnson began to suffer back problems and was released after the 1988 season. He played four more years—two with the Indianapolis Colts and two with the Houston Oilers. A Pro Bowler in 1978, Johnson was inducted into the Packers Hall of Fame in 1997.

DEFENSIVE TACKLES

The Candidates

Dave Hanner
Gilbert Brown
Henry Jordan
Cal Hubbard

If defensive tackle isn't the most thankless position in football, it's certainly in the top two. Whether it's the 4-3 defensive alignment (two tackles, two ends, and three linebackers) or the increasingly more popular and versatile 3-4 (two defensive ends, a nose tackle, and four linebackers), the tackle is usually on the bottom of the pile at the end of most plays.

It takes a player of a certain stature, both physically and mentally, to play the tackle spot, and while we have stretched the rules a little on this position for our team, the effect is the same. It requires a player of size and strength who understands that he's often the key to slowing down the offensive running game. And if the running game isn't working, the options for the offense decrease while they improve for the defense.

So we're going to feature both nose tackles as well as tackles from the more traditional defense. But make no mistake, they can all do the job, no matter what is required.

DAVE HANNER

Has anyone given more years to the Green Bay Packers organization than Dave Hanner? In a word—no. Not only did he play 13 seasons deep in the trenches at tackle for some pretty bad, and then some incredibly good, Packers teams, he would go on to spend the next three decades as a coach and scout for the organization that did so much for him and, in turn, for which he provided so much.

A fifth-round draft pick in 1952 out of the University of Arkansas, he was immediately tagged with the nickname that stayed with him the rest of his life—"Hawg."

But he was more than a nickname. Tough and strong, he was almost impossible for offensive linemen to push off the line of scrimmage. And while he was rarely a threat to rush the quarterback, he was always around to stop running backs and was especially good at sniffing out screen passes and shutting them down.

Hanner was a two-time All-Pro in his early years for some mediocre teams, but when Vince Lombardi came in as head coach in 1959 Hanner found a second wind. Lombardi put him at left tackle and he flourished in between two Hall of Famers in Henry Jordan and Willie Davis and was a key member of Green Bay's 1961 and '62 NFL title teams.

He retired (well, Lombardi told him to retire) after the 1964 season and immediately latched on as the Packers' defensive line coach. In 1971 he was promoted to defensive coordinator by Dan Devine, and from 1975 to 1979 he was assistant head coach and defensive coordinator under Bart Starr.

Dave Hanner's 1954 Bowman card

He left the Packers for two years to join the Chicago Bears, but in 1982 he was back in Green Bay under Starr as quality control coordinator and then as a scout starting in 1983.

He retired at the end of the 1996 season after the Packers' Super Bowl XXXI win having spent, in all, 44 years with the organization—13 as a player, 16 as a coach, and 15 as a scout. His tenure with the team is the longest in franchise history.

Hanner was inducted into the Packers Hall of Fame in 1974 and he died in 2008.

GILBERT BROWN

There was a time when Gilbert Brown was, literally, in the middle of everything for a Packers defense. Called a right tackle for his first few seasons, he was, and always will be, a nose tackle. At 6-foot-3 and weighing (depending on who you wanted to believe) 340 to 380 pounds, Brown was remarkably nimble, surprisingly quick, and a force in the middle of some of the best defenses in team history.

And he remains, even today, one of the most popular players for a franchise that has had its fair share.

But he began his Packers career as something of an afterthought.

A third-round draft choice of the Minnesota Vikings in 1993 out of the University of Kansas, Brown's weight was a concern and late in training camp he was cut.

The Packers, then in their second season under Mike Holmgren, were in need of defensive help and thought Brown might be an intriguing addition.

Defensive coordinator Fritz Shurmur saw just how quick Brown was for a guy his size and realized he could be a force inside. Shurmur knew how important defensive linemen were and he knew that if Brown could be a part of stopping the run, the rest of the defense could excel.

And he did that superbly.

In 1996, the first season he was healthy enough to play a full schedule, he helped anchor one of the best, if most under-rated, defenses in NFL history. In fact, that defense allowed just 19 touchdowns all season—one of the best performances in NFL history.

And Brown was one of the emotional leaders. Indeed, every time he'd make a tackle or force a big play, he would mimic digging, emphatically, a grave. He was, after all, "the Gravedigger" for rival running backs, and his routine electri-fied Packers fans.

He never earned any league honors for that season as the Packers rolled to a Super Bowl title, but the Packers knew all too well how critical he was to their success. They also learned how important loyalty was to the big guy.

Brown was a free agent after the 1996 season, easily his best as a pro, and the Jacksonville Jaguars offered him a staggering deal—three years, $9 million.

But Brown turned it down to sign a three-year deal with the Packers for what amounted to $1 million less than the Jag-uars' offer.

He said at the time it was not a difficult decision. Simply, he felt comfortable in Green Bay and with the Packers.

He remained a force on the defense, helping the Packers to a second straight Super Bowl in 1997, but a knee injury led to his release prior to the start of the 2000 season.

Convinced his career wasn't over, he went on a major work-out routine and reportedly lost 40 pounds. He was determined to come back.

And in the spring of 2001, a 325-pound Gilbert Brown was re-signed by the Packers.

He played well for three more seasons in the middle of the Packers defense, but in a 2003 preseason game he suffered a serious arm injury and instead of undergoing surgery, he tried to play through it.

He was released after the 2003 season even though he remained convinced he could still play.

And though he has moved on from that disappointment, he has never quite forgiven coach and general manager Mike Sherman, who made the decision to let him go. It was a decision Brown did not agree with.

Brown thought about playing elsewhere, but after so many years in Green Bay, it wasn't something he was excited about doing.

He has remained in the Green Bay area, coaching and working with his foundation to support children's charities.

In his career he played 125 games with 103 starts, and his 15 playoff games are still second in team history behind Brett Favre.

Brown finished with 292 tackles and seven quarterback sacks, and he was inducted into the Packers Hall of Fame in 2008.

Henry Jordan

There are not many statistics that define Henry Jordan.

Tackles? Not kept back then. Quarterback sacks? They were years away from being a statistic. Quarterback hurries and tackles for loss? Not even close.

But numbers never did define who Jordan was and what he meant to the Packers. In his first 12 seasons, he missed only two games. He played in six NFL Championship Games and two Super Bowls and was a four-time Pro Bowler and five-time All-Pro selection.

And in 1995 he was inducted into the Pro Football Hall of Fame.

He may have been difficult to define, but his play spoke volumes.

"He had extreme quickness," said his former teammate, guard Jerry Kramer. "He was small for a defensive tackle, but he had great quickness and he survived on his quickness. He was also pretty strong, but his quickness was outstanding."

With his receding hairline, Jordan looked more like the neighborhood dentist. But he was a terrific athlete—an NCAA champion wrestler and a fifth-round draft choice of the Cleveland Browns in 1957, whom he helped lead to a conference title.

But, in one of his first moves as the new coach of the Packers prior to the 1959 season, Vince Lombardi traded a fourth-round draft pick to the Browns for Jordan. In Green Bay he thrived.

As Kramer said, even in this era of the NFL, at 6-foot-2, 250 pounds, Jordan was an undersized defensive tackle. But he was everywhere on every play, using his quickness to beat rival offensive linemen.

Affable and quotable, Jordan was a frequent interview subject for reporters and could be found on many off-season speaking engagements.

He is generally credited with the famous quote about how Lombardi treated his players.

"He treated us all the same," Jordan said. "Like dogs."

Kramer remembered a 1967 playoff game against Los Angeles when Jordan was credited with 3½ sacks of Rams quarterback Roman Gabriel as well as a fumble recovery (for his career, Jordan recovered a remarkable 20 fumbles).

The irony is that a few months earlier, as 1967 training camp opened, Jordan went to Lombardi with his playbook. He told his coach that he had lost the passion to play and did not want to stick around to simply collect a paycheck when there were other players who could step in and do the job.

Lombardi told his star tackle to take some time to think about his decision and, in what was something less than a surprise, Jordan did indeed agree to return to play. And in some ways, it may have been his best season. It was the year of the "Ice Bowl" and the year that the Packers beat the Oakland Raiders in Super Bowl II, winning their third straight NFL title.

He continued to play in both 1968 and 1969, but the Packers juggernaut was collapsing through age and injury and retirement. Even Lombardi had moved on.

In 1969 Jordan played only five games due to injury, and after that season he, too, retired.

He settled in the Milwaukee area and became a driving force in the creation of Milwaukee's annual summer music festival, Summerfest. He was inducted into the Packers Hall of Fame in 1975.

But in February 1977, after a workout at a local Milwaukee health club, Jordan suffered a heart attack and died. He was just 42.

Gone and perhaps somewhat forgotten, Henry Jordan epitomized toughness and agility and is one of the names from the Packers' golden age that should continue to resonate.

CAL HUBBARD

Back in those days when the NFL was still figuring out what it was and what it might one day be, Cal Hubbard decided to try something different.

He was a mountain of a man (at least in the NFL of the 1920s and 30s). At 6-foot-2 and 270 pounds, he quickly developed a reputation for his quickness and power and in the ultimate compliment to a defensive lineman, many opponents believed he was simply impossible to block.

He got his start with the New York Giants in 1927 and decided to take a new approach toward playing defense. So in one game, he stood up and stepped off the line of scrimmage, providing him a better opportunity to stop a running back. Little did he know at the time, but that move was the first nod toward a new position that would be known as a linebacker.

Not that Hubbard needed any more of an advantage; he was already known by many as a "big man in a small world."

In 1929 Hubbard was sold to Curly Lambeau's Packers and he continued to wreak havoc on the NFL. He teamed up with fellow lineman Mike Michalske, who also tipped the scales at around 270 pounds, to form the most devastating defensive front in the game.

Led by that defense, the Packers won league championships in 1929, 1930, and 1931, and Hubbard was often singled out for his dominant play.

The accolades rolled in even as he played. He was often compared to the Empire State Building when he stood on the field. A New York columnist said he could spill rival backs like bowling pins. Mel Hein, a Hall of Fame center, said Hubbard was the greatest tackle he ever played against.

And George Halas, who had formed the Chicago Bears at the same time Lambeau had created the Packers, said simply, "There never was a better lineman than that big lineman."

Hubbard played for the Packers until 1933, then retired to become a coach at Texas A&M. He was lured back by Lambeau to play one more season in 1935 as a player/coach.

In 1936 he became an American League baseball umpire and at midseason was given his release by the Packers. He finished his football career playing first for Pittsburgh and then the Giants before embarking on a 15-year career as a Major League umpire.

In 1954 he became supervisor of umpires, a position he held until 1970.

Indeed, Hubbard was a star in two different sports.

In the NFL, he was named to the league's 50th and 75th Anniversary Teams as well as the league's All-Decade Team for the 1920s. He was also named to the Packers' 50th Anniversary Team and its All-Iron Man Era Team.

He was inducted into the Pro Football Hall of Fame in 1963 and the Packers Hall of Fame in 1970, and he was inducted into the Baseball Hall of Fame in 1976.

The final word goes to Bo McMillin, a college football star and an NFL player and head coach who said of Hubbard, "The greatest player who ever lived was Cal Hubbard, lineman or back, college or professional."

A big statement for a big man.

AND THE WINNERS ARE ...

The truth is, the Packers have not been blessed with great defensive tackles since the late 1960s.

So we needed to dig deep in the team's history to find the players who could make this all-star team special.

Neither of our choices could likely play in today's NFL—but that's not the point. As we've said, this is about who could play when they played.

So we're going with one true tackle whose agility and intelligence and quickness helped make the Packers the dominant team of the 1960s: **Henry Jordan**.

It's the same with the other tackle spot. In the 1920s and early '30s, no one dominated the defensive line like **Cal Hubbard**. And at that time, when the league featured its first set of stars—all of whom played on both offense and defense—that domination matters. That later generations may not know his name or recite his statistics is due to the vagaries of time. But to listen to his contemporaries speak of him in awe is all the evidence needed. He was one of the best..

Had Gilbert Brown played longer and, frankly, earned league honors (he did not), he might well have cracked this lineup. In his prime he was as pure a run-stopper as the league knew and, as with Hubbard and Jordan in their own eras, he was a key to that dominant Packers defense in the mid-'90s.

DEFENSIVE TACKLES WHO DID NOT MAKE THE CUT

Kenny Clark's story is still being written. But if injuries stay away and the team's circumstances improve, Clark has the potential to be one of the great nose tackles in team history. The UCLA product was Green Bay's first-round draft pick in 2016 and he stepped in to become a force on a defense that has struggled in recent seasons. In three seasons he has already posted more than 130 tackles from a position where tackles can be hard to come by. More impressively, he has 10½ quarterback sacks, including six in the 2018 season, a campaign in which he earned Pro Bowl recognition.

Ryan Pickett was another of the nose tackles who could change a game. And he had been one for five seasons in St. Louis, toiling almost anonymously for a Rams team that was far better known for its high-powered offense than its defense. He joined the Packers as a free agent in 2006 and was a stout, dependable tackle for eight seasons. He played in 119 games (starting 113) and recorded 198 solo tackles and 3½ quarterback sacks. He finished his solid career in 2014 with the Houston Texans, but he was also part of two Super Bowl champion teams—one in St. Louis and one in Green Bay.

Originally a fifth-round draft pick of the Tampa Bay Buccaneers in 1992, **Santana Dotson** seemed to be in the perfect spot, posting 10 quarterback sacks from his tackle position (which would be a career high), and being named NFC Defensive Rookie of the Year for an up-and-coming young team. But after three years it was time for Dotson to move on, and while he was being sought by the Minnesota Vikings and Green Bay Packers, Dotson knew the choice was no choice at all. Rumor and innuendo about Dotson's commitment to football dogged him but didn't concern the Packers. They saw in Dotson a veteran tackle who could get to the quarterback, stop the run, and provide an excellent complement to what may well have been the best defensive line in football. And Dotson reestablished himself as a quality tackle. In that Super Bowl–winning season of 1996 he finished with 5½ sacks, and over the course of the next five seasons he posted a total of 26 sacks, 158 tackles, and 107 assists. He also forced six fumbles. In 1999 he missed his first game as a Packer, in 2000 he suffered a torn quadriceps muscle, and in 2001 he was slowed with a neck injury. After being released by Green Bay in 2002, he signed with the Washington Redskins but injuries continued and he retired.

LINEBACKERS

The Candidates

Ray Nitschke
John Anderson
Dave Robinson
Clay Matthews

This isn't going to be easy. The linebacker position requires so much in the way of intelligence, speed, strength, agility, and athleticism. In many ways, the linebacker position is perhaps the one that has changed the least in the always-changing NFL.

The goal is the same: Flow to the running back, fill a hole, and stop him. Blitz the quarterback and bring him down. Fall back in coverage and make a play on a wide receiver.

Our candidates, like those for every other position on this team, come from various eras in which they were among the best at what they did.

RAY NITSCHKE
In a game often given to hyperbole, this is one time the claim fits the facts: Ray Nitschke is the best linebacker the Green Bay Packers have ever had. Maybe the best they will ever have.

Ray Nitschke in 1966

"I really prepared to play," Nitschke said after he retired. "I was always ready. There wasn't anything on the field I wasn't prepared for."

And it showed. For 15 seasons, Nitschke (even the name "Nitschke" is tough) was, in a very real sense, the soul and personality of Packers teams that featured some of the best talent of the time. And he was, literally, in the middle of Green Bay's five championships in the 1960s.

But it wasn't always that way. A third-round draft pick in 1958, Nitschke was a Chicago kid who played football at the University of Illinois and dreamed of being drafted by his hometown Bears.

And while many Packers fans can recall Nitschke as the monster at middle linebacker, he didn't actually become a full-time starter until 1962.

As a rookie, he did start ahead of Tom Bettis but lost that spot due to his tendency to make too many mistakes. He alternated with Bettis for several years, missing half of the 1961 season when he was called up to active duty in the army.

Some Packers teased Nitschke, giving him the nickname "the Judge" because he spent so much time on the bench.

Finally, in 1962 Lombardi traded Bettis and gave the job full time to Nitschke who, the coach said, had improved his game dramatically. And Nitschke responded.

In the 1962 NFL Championship he was named the defensive MVP, recovering two fumbles and deflecting a pass that was intercepted as Green Bay beat the New York Giants, 16–7.

And for years, he was the force that rival offenses knew they had to avoid but, more often than not, could not. For Nitschke, the philosophy was simple.

"You want them to have respect for you when they run a play at you," he once said to Bud Lea of the *Milwaukee Journal Sentinel*. "You want them to be a little shy and a little shier the next time. You want them to remember you're in there."

Nitschke anchored the defense for three more championships and took his place as one of the most beloved, and devoted, Packers of all time.

Which made it that much more difficult, both for Nitschke and the fans who loved him, to say goodbye.

Nitschke was still a shrine to the glory days of Packers football, but a new decade was dawning and those days were long gone. By 1971 many of the players who had made the Packers so formidable had either retired or moved on to other teams. Vince Lombardi was dead, and time had finally caught up to the seemingly indestructible middle linebacker.

In 1971 coach Dan Devine decided to move second-year player Jim Carter to middle linebacker, replacing Nitschke. Football-wise, it seemed to make sense, but it was a public relations disaster.

Fans were outraged that their legend and, really, the last tie to the golden years had been replaced by a kid. Nitschke wasn't thrilled either.

He overtly complained about the demotion, but nearly every game that season, when it was time for the defense to go on the field, Nitschke would stretch as though he were warming up to come in. When Carter took the field, fans greeted him with a torrent of boos.

And Carter, a Pro Bowler in his own right, heard it all—and it hurt.

Finally, in 1972, Nitschke retired after 15 seasons. But Ray Nitschke was hardly forgotten.

He was a five-time All-Pro and a Pro Bowler in 1964. He finished with 25 interceptions and his 20 career fumble recoveries is still second all-time in team history behind Willie Davis. He was also named to the NFL's 50th and 75th Anniversary Teams and, perhaps most important to him, he played 190 games, still in the top five in team history.

He was inducted into both the Pro Football Hall of Fame and Packers Hall of Fame in 1978, and in 1983 his number 66 became just the fourth Packer number retired, joining at the time Tony Canadeo (3), Don Hutson (14), and Bart Starr (15).

Nitschke became a fixture in Green Bay after his playing days ended. He did community events by the hundreds over the years and reveled in being a Green Bay Packer. His phone number was even listed in the local phone book.

And while he agonized over the Packers' struggles in the intervening years, when they won Super Bowl XXXI in January 1997, he wept in joy.

In March 1998, while on vacation in Florida, he suffered a heart attack and died at the age of 61. His passing was front-page news around Wisconsin and the thoughts were all the same: His like will never be seen again.

JOHN ANDERSON

John Anderson still remembers the surreal feeling of not only being a first-round NFL draft pick but a first-round draft pick of the team he had idolized his entire life.

A native of Waukesha, Wisconsin, outside Milwaukee, Anderson had spent his youth in the backyard pretending he was legendary Packers quarterback Bart Starr. On this day in 1978, Starr was now the Packers coach and phoning Anderson to tell him how excited he was to have him on the team.

"It was pretty exciting," Anderson told Martin Hendricks of the *Milwaukee Journal Sentinel*.

Understated, to say the least. But that was Anderson, who played 12 seasons for the Packers, piling up numbers quietly and without fanfare because, in the end, that was his job.

In truth, he played for teams that ranged from mediocre to terrible, but he never let that impact his play. Every down he gave it his best, and Packers fans loved him for it and teammates respected him for it.

Yet he knew immediately that, as a Wisconsin kid and a first-round pick after a stellar college career at the University of Michigan, expectations were high.

"It's a somber thought," Anderson told Hendricks. "If I wash out in Dallas, no one cares. My family and friends expected big things. But what if it doesn't happen? What if I wash out? In my home state, I didn't want to be a failure."

He wasn't. Indeed, in his first 14 games he intercepted five passes, starting a pro career no one could have dreamed about.

But in a December game against Tampa Bay, Anderson broke his left arm, ending his season. Then he broke the same arm two more times over the next two seasons, forcing him to miss 15 games total. A bone graft in 1980 finally allowed him to get back on the field on a consistent basis.

The team's results were not as consistent as Anderson's performance. He would end up playing for three coaches—Starr, Forrest Gregg, and Lindy Infante—and he'd be a part of only three winning teams and four others that went 8-8. He would be involved in only two playoff games.

Still, Anderson was selected as Green Bay's most valuable defensive player three times. His 1,020 tackles are still a team record, and his 25 interceptions are tied with Ray Nitschke for the most by a Packers linebacker. He was a member of the NFL's 1980s All-Decade Team, and he was inducted into the Packers Hall of Fame in 1996.

Anderson went on to become a sports anchor in Milwaukee as well as an elementary school teacher. He remains in education as of 2018 and is proud not only of his Packers career but the fact that he left on his terms.

"No one had to show me the door," he said to the *Journal Sentinel*. "I walked away healthy and with many friends. But I wish we'd won more in the '80s."

Dave Robinson

Years later, Dave Robinson still laughs at the story from the 1966 NFL Championship, when the Packers held off the Dallas Cowboys in the final minutes to win their second straight title.

All Packers fans, and more than a few Cowboys fans, recall how Cowboys quarterback Don Meredith threw an interception in the end zone in the final seconds to seal the Packers' 34–27 win.

But while safety Tom Brown gets credit for the interception, it was linebacker Dave Robinson who thundered in on Meredith, forcing him to make a hurried throw that Brown grabbed easily.

After the game, coach Vince Lombardi congratulated Robinson on the instinctive play and pressure but later told him he would have to lower Robinson's game grade (a key element that all players looked at after each game) because he hadn't followed his assignment.

"Ha!" Robinson would say later. "That was Lombardi."

It was also Robinson—a tall, athletic linebacker who always seemed to be around the ball and making huge plays.

One rival quarterback once said that throwing over Robinson, who was 6-foot-3 and 240 pounds and who possessed unusually long arms, was like trying to throw over the Empire State Building.

For 10 seasons he was a rock at the left linebacker spot, and after a wait that many football observers thought was far too long, he was inducted into the Pro Football Hall of Fame in 2013.

"I finally made it and I'm here forever," Robinson said in his induction speech. "The thing about the Hall of Fame is it's the closest thing a football player can get to immortality."

And Robinson will forever be known as another member of those remarkable Packers teams that seemed to include Hall of Famers around every corner.

"I was very fortunate to play in Green Bay," he said.

He came to the Packers with big expectations. The Packers were already a force in 1963, having come off their second straight title, in 1962, with a 16–7 win over the New York Giants. It was a draft that featured several other starters including Tom Brown, defensive end Lionel Aldridge, and tight end Marv Fleming, but Robinson was the one who was expected to make an immediate impact.

A great athlete at Penn State, Robinson was moved from defensive end in college to linebacker and after a year behind Dan Currie, he stepped in as the starter and never left. And he soon showed that he had a nose for the big play.

His favorite game came in December 1965 against the Baltimore Colts.

Battling for a playoff spot, the Packers faced the Colts in foggy Baltimore. Late in the first half, with the Packers leading just 14–13, Baltimore had a chance to score after a Green Bay turnover.

But Robinson intercepted a pass in the end zone and returned it 87 yards to the Colts' 10. Green Bay scored on the next play to turn the tide and win easily.

The two teams met again two weeks later in a playoff for the Western Conference title.

A late field goal, still debated to this day as to whether it went through the uprights, tied the game for the Packers. They won with another three-pointer in overtime. The next week the Packers dominated the Cleveland Browns to win their third title. The next year, in a classic postseason win, Robinson harassed Dallas Cowboys quarterback Don Meredith into an interception.

Robinson starred in both Super Bowl wins, but in 1970 he ruptured an Achilles tendon and missed 10 games. He came back to play two more seasons before he was traded to the Washington Redskins in 1973.

He would go on to play two more solid seasons in Washington before retiring after the 1974 season. But he knew he'd always be a Green Bay Packer, no matter what other uniform he wore.

Robinson was named to three Pro Bowls, was a three-time All-Pro, and was inducted into the Packers Hall of Fame in 1982.

CLAY MATTHEWS

He blew into Green Bay as a first-round draft pick from the University of Southern California in 2009, which (in a convoluted fashion peculiar to the NFL) was the pick the Packers

Clay Matthews
AMY ANDERSON VIA WIKIMEDIA COMMONS

had acquired from the New York Jets the previous summer for Brett Favre. Matthews wasted no time showing that not only did he belong in the NFL, he was practically indispensable to the Packers.

He has toiled for 10 seasons (through 2018) in Green Bay, battling injuries, team inconsistency, and a seemingly endless position change from outside to inside linebacker and has always done the job asked of him.

Matthews made his presence felt that first season, scoring a touchdown on a strip and fumble recovery of Minnesota Vikings running back Adrian Peterson in October. He recorded 10 sacks and 51 tackles, and earned a Pro Bowl spot, the first Packers rookie to do so since James Lofton in 1978.

As offenses learned how dangerous and versatile Matthews was, new blocking schemes, directly designed to stop him, were implemented. Yet he continued to wreak havoc on rivals.

On September 28, 2017, Matthews took over as the Packers' all-time sack leader when he brought down Chicago Bears quarterback Mike Glennon.

And though his numbers have slipped in recent seasons due to nagging injuries, he remains a pivotal force on the Packers defense.

Through the 2018 season, Matthews has piled up 85½ sacks and his 482 tackles are among the most in team history.

But time moves on, and in the spring of 2019 Matthews signed a two-year free agent contract with the Los Angeles Rams, ending his 10-year stint in Green Bay.

He was a six-time Pro Bowler with the Packers, a three-time All-Pro, and the Professional Football Writers Association Defensive Player of the Year in 2010 when, from his outside linebacker spot, he racked up 13½ sacks, four pass deflections, two forced fumbles, and an interception as the Packers won the Super Bowl.

Certain to be inducted into the Packers Hall of Fame, he is also a strong candidate to be yet another Green Bay addition to the Pro Football Hall of Fame one day.

AND THE WINNERS ARE . . .

It's another photo finish, and if the decision were made to keep four linebackers, everything would be a lot easier.

Instead . . .

The three linebackers who make this all-star team bring very similar talents that resulted in varying degrees of success for their team.

Ray Nitschke, **Dave Robinson**, and **Clay Matthews**, just edging out John Anderson after some back-and-forth, are the three who make this team.

Nitschke is a no-brainer. He was one of the premier linebackers of his era and a huge part of the defense that helped the Packers to five championships in the 1960s. Ditto for Dave Robinson. They were two of the greatest linebackers who ever played.

The third choice of Matthews over Anderson may have been the toughest decision of this entire team. Both put in many quality seasons for the Packers. Both excelled during sometimes trying circumstances. Both have given back to the community that embraced them. But Matthews's sheer numbers are difficult to ignore. And, yes, he was a key element on a Super Bowl–winning team.

Linebackers Who Did Not Make the Cut

Tim Harris was a force of nature who burned brightly for five seasons in Green Bay (1986–90). Known for his brash attitude and ability to get under the skin of opponents (and some teammates, too) with his nonstop trash-talking, he also backed it up with a rare combination of speed and strength. At 6-foot-5, 240 pounds, he first started as a rookie under coach Forrest Gregg in 1986. When Lindy Infante took over in 1988, the new coach said, "I'll take 11 Tim Harrises on my team any day." Harris led the Packers in sacks in all five of his seasons in Green Bay, including 19½ in 1989, the year he was named to the Pro Bowl. He finished his Packers career with 55 sacks, still fourth-best in team history. Due to a contract dispute the Packers traded Harris to the San Francisco 49ers, where he won a Super Bowl ring before going on to the Philadelphia Eagles and back to the 49ers to finish before retiring in 1995. But football was hard on Harris, who told Martin Hendricks of the *Milwaukee Journal Sentinel* in 2014 that he has endured 32 surgeries and is on NFL-sanctioned disability.

Dan Currie was the Packers' first-round selection in the 1958 draft, which is widely considered the best draft in team history. That draft netted, along with Currie, Hall of Famers Jim Taylor, Ray Nitschke, and Jerry Kramer, and had his career not been derailed by a knee injury, Currie could well have been added to that list. He played six seasons with the Packers (1958–64), and after a disastrous rookie season that saw the Packers go 1-10-1, Vince Lombardi came in and the story changed. "He was easy to work for as long as you did your job," Currie told the *Milwaukee Journal Sentinel* about Lombardi. "He was a guy you couldn't B.S. He was exactly what he was. He was an educator and he was very smart." Currie was named All-Pro three times and went to one Pro Bowl, but with a future Hall of Famer, Dave Robinson, waiting in the wings, Lombardi traded Currie to the Los Angeles Rams for Carroll Dale. Currie remained a lifelong Packers fan and was inducted into the Packers Hall of Fame in 1984. He died in 2017.

A third-round draft pick in 1953, **Bill Forester** actually got his start as a defensive end, but after three seasons he was moved to linebacker. He played on the Packers' first two championship teams under Lombardi before retiring in 1963 after 11 quality seasons. He was a three-time All-Pro and a four-time Pro Bowler and was also defensive captain for five seasons. He was a Pro Football Hall of Fame nominee. Perhaps his greatest individual claim to fame was that he sacked Colts quarterback Johnny Unitas four times in one half of a game in 1962—though the statistic was not kept back then. He was inducted into the Packers Hall of Fame in 1974.

Tagged with the perfect nickname of "Mad Dog," fan favorite **Mike Douglass** prowled the Packers defense from 1978 to 1985. A fifth-round draft pick from San Diego State, Douglass was everywhere on the field for some good, some bad, and some indifferent Packers teams. His 967 tackles are still third in team history and he was voted team defensive MVP in 1980 and 1981. He finished his career with 10 interceptions and led the Packers in quarterback sacks in 1984 with nine. He was inducted into the Packers Hall of Fame in 2003.

CORNERBACKS

The Candidates
Herb Adderley
Mark Lee
Charles Woodson

It is the loneliest position on either side of the ball. It is often said a cornerback lives on an island, facing a speedy, athletic receiver who knows where he's going, with often no other defender around to help. It's one-on-one, and may the best man win. Too often, it's the receiver and the only recourse for a beaten cornerback is to forget what happened and seek redemption on the next play.

Perhaps the greatest cornerback in team history didn't even begin, or end, his career in Green Bay. But in the time he was here, he was a force that could alter the course of games. He came to Green Bay seeking a new opportunity and found everything he was looking for—and more.

HERB ADDERLEY
It was almost the greatest mistake Vince Lombardi made as head coach of the Green Bay Packers. When the Packers selected Herb Adderley with their first pick in the 1961 draft,

they thought that since Adderley had been such a good running back at Michigan State, he'd be a good running back in Green Bay.

But circumstances changed all that. The Packers were set at running back with Paul Hornung and Jim Taylor, and while Lombardi thought about keeping the new kid there, it occurred to him Adderley might be better elsewhere.

"I was too stubborn to switch him to defense until I had to," Lombardi once said. "Now when I think of what Adderley means to our defense, it scares me to think of how I almost mishandled him."

But it took a midseason injury to starting cornerback Hank Gremminger for Lombardi to see the light and move in Adderley as an emergency starter. And once he did, a good defense became almost impenetrable. Adderley eventually became one of the leaders of the defense, not to mention one of the top cornerbacks in the history of the NFL. But there was one accolade that meant the most to him.

"Lombardi had certain players who he'd call into his office and talk to, others he'd talk to on the field or in the locker room," Adderley said during his Pro Football Hall of Fame induction speech in 1980. "One thing I remember he said to me: He said I was the best cornerback he'd ever seen. In front of the whole team he said I was the best athlete. I'll always remember that."

In his nine seasons with the Packers, Adderley intercepted 39 passes and never had fewer than three interceptions a season. He also returned seven for touchdowns. In 1962, his first full season as a starter, he picked off seven passes. In 1965 he had six interceptions, bringing back three for touchdowns and leading the league with 175 interception return yards.

He did the same thing in 1969, his final season with the Packers, when he intercepted five passes for a league-best 169 yards.

In the Super Bowl II win over the Oakland Raiders, Adderley returned an interception 61 yards for a score, the only interception returned for a touchdown in the first 10 Super Bowls.

"He was just always in the right place all the time," said Packers quarterback Bart Starr. "Lombardi was right. He was also the best cornerback I'd ever seen, too, and I'm glad he was on our team."

He was also one the league's top kickoff returners. In 1963 he averaged nearly 30 yards per return. And in eight seasons returning kicks for Green Bay, he averaged nearly 26 yards a return, bringing two back for touchdowns.

In 1970, with the Packers' dynasty ending, Adderley was traded to the new dynasty, the Dallas Cowboys, where he played in two more Super Bowls before retiring in 1972.

Adderley was a five-time Pro Bowler and a seven-time All-Pro and was named to the NFL's All-Decade Team of the 1960s. A year after his induction into the Pro Football Hall in Fame, Adderley was named to the Packers Hall of Fame.

Adderley returned to his native Philadelphia after his playing days and did some college coaching. He still lives there.

MARK LEE

Sometimes, longevity has to count. Through trades and contract disputes and injuries, careers come and go and end, sometimes without warning.

Exhibit A is Mark Lee, a tough and dedicated cornerback who played 11 seasons for the Packers and, while usually covering the opponent's top receiver week in and week out, missed exactly eight games.

Lee was a second-round draft pick in 1980 out of the University of Washington. Though not imposing in size (he was 5-foot-11 and 180 pounds), he had good instincts and athleticism that allowed him to crack the starting lineup as a rookie while also serving as the team's main punt returner.

In his first full season as a starter in 1981, he intercepted a team-high six passes. He would go on to rack up 31 career picks, including a career-high nine in 1986. Lee still ranks eighth overall in team history and second among cornerbacks in interceptions. He also forced nine fumbles and recovered seven.

The only blemish on his career was that in his 11 seasons, from 1980 to 1990, the Packers managed to participate in just two playoff games.

"We didn't have a whole bunch of winning seasons," he said. "But the fans were always behind us."

Lee finished his career splitting time with the New Orleans Saints and San Francisco 49ers in 1991 before retiring.

And while Lee never had any illusions about earning induction into the Pro Football Hall of Fame, he had long hoped that his time and dedication to the Packers would eventually earn him a spot in the team's shrine.

But that call never came, and he assumed after more than 20 years that it never would.

"My mom always told me, 'Better late than never,'" Lee said with a smile.

That's because in 2017 the call did come, and Lee was inducted into the Packers Hall of Fame.

"This means a lot," he said in his induction speech. "You always play to be the last team standing and to hold the Lombardi Trophy for winning the Super Bowl. But this means a lot to me. I'll wear this as a badge of honor for the rest of my life."

CHARLES WOODSON

He didn't start his career with the Packers and he didn't finish it with the Packers. But the seven seasons in between when he was a Packer? Oh, my.

In those seven seasons, 2006–12, Woodson changed the culture of the Packers defense as he finally fulfilled his dream of winning a Super Bowl.

Woodson was no kid when he joined the Packers. A Heisman Trophy winner at the University of Michigan, he was originally a first-round draft pick of the Oakland Raiders in 1998,

Charles Woodson in 2009
MIKE MORBECK VIA WIKIMEDIA COMMONS

where he developed a reputation as a great cornerback with a sometimes lousy attitude.

After eight seasons with the Raiders he decided to test the free agent market, and instead of being flooded with offers as he expected, just one came—from Green Bay.

And while it wasn't his first choice to come to the frozen wilds of Wisconsin, he also knew he didn't have many other options. What resulted was a love affair between the Packers and Woodson.

Already a veteran who knew how to win and how to prepare, he helped school many young cornerbacks over the years while he rediscovered his love of the game, which had eventually abandoned him in Oakland.

In his seven seasons with the Packers, he intercepted an incredible 38 passes, returning nine for touchdowns. In fact, he had at least one interception for a touchdown in every season with the Packers except his last.

In 2009 he led the league with nine interceptions (three for touchdowns), and he did it again in 2011 when he intercepted seven passes. He also returned punts and played occasionally on offense when asked. And in his final season, he moved to strong safety.

In February 2011 he was Green Bay's starting corner in Super Bowl XLV, but he broke his shoulder late in the first half and was lost for the rest of the game. It was his emotional and tear-filled halftime speech to his teammates that many of them credit for helping the Packers surge to the win.

In 2013 he returned to the Raiders and played three more years before retiring. He is a shoo-in for induction into the Pro Football Hall of Fame, and though he has yet to get into the Packers Hall of Fame, he has a spot reserved there, too.

The argument rages these days about the greatest free agent signing in team history. Most people still believe the signing of the peerless defensive end Reggie White in 1993 is number one because of what it meant to the image and future of the franchise. But a strong case can be made for Charles Woodson as well. His experience and talent and ability to change a game were unmatched.

AND THE WINNERS ARE . . .

When there is a Packer from the 1960s involved, it's usually a good bet to include him on any all-star team. So it is with **Herb Adderley**, who was such a steady and dominating force in the defensive backfield along with the underrated Bob Jeter, who in his eight years with the Packers (1963–70) was an awfully good player in his own right. Adderley is joined by **Charles Woodson**, whose seven seasons in Green Bay helped him recharge a career that was on the way down. He was a leader by example in every sense of the word.

CORNERBACKS WHO DID NOT MAKE THE CUT

Speaking of **Bob Jeter**, he was a superb complement to Adderley and another key member of that 1960s defense. He was the Packers' second-round draft pick in 1960 but went to the Canadian Football League as a running back for the British Columbia Lions for two seasons. He joined the Packers' taxi squad in 1962 and was tried at wide receiver for two more seasons before settling in as the cornerback opposite Adderley. He flourished in that role. In six full seasons at cornerback he intercepted 23 passes, including a career-best eight in 1967. He also returned two for touchdowns in 1966. He was named to two Pro Bowls, was an All-Pro one time, and was inducted into the Packers

Hall of Fame in 1985. He died of a heart attack at age 71 in 2008.

All told, **Ken Ellis** played for six NFL teams in his 10-year career, which spanned from 1970 to 1979. But while he played for the Cleveland Browns, Houston Oilers, Los Angeles Rams, Miami Dolphins, and Detroit Lions, it was his first six seasons with the Packers that most remember. He was always around the ball and always making plays. He was drafted as a wide receiver but when Herb Adderley held out, coach Phil Bengtson asked Ellis if he wanted to try defense. It was the right decision. In just 83 games he intercepted 20 passes, returning three for touchdowns, and forced seven fumbles and recovered six. He also returned one punt for a touchdown and, in the first one ever in the NFL, he brought back a missed field goal for a score. But in 1976 he also held out for a better contract and walked out of training camp twice. He was eventually dealt to the Oilers for, among others, quarterback Lynn Dickey. Ellis was a two-time Pro Bowler and All-Pro and was inducted into the Packers Hall of Fame in 1998.

Willie Buchanon from San Diego State was one of two first-round draft picks in 1972. The other was Green Bay native and University of Nebraska quarterback Jerry Tagge. Suffice it to say one of those picks worked out superbly. In that 1972 season, when the Packers made it back to the playoffs for the first time in five years, the rookie Buchanon was a huge part of it. He was named NFC Defensive Rookie of the Year, intercepting four passes and helping solidify a secondary that was one of the best in the league. Over the next three seasons, injuries forced him to miss 20 games but in 1978, when he knew he'd be playing out his contract option, Buchanon had the season of his life. He returned with the Packers for a game in his hometown of San Diego and intercepted four passes, one for a touchdown. He had nine interceptions that season and was named a Pro Bowler and an All-Pro. The next season he signed with the Chargers, where he played four seasons before retiring. In his seven seasons with the Packers, he posted 21 interceptions. He was inducted into the Packers Hall of Fame in 1993.

SAFETIES

The Candidates
Bobby Dillon
LeRoy Butler
Willie Wood

They are the last line of the defense, often the best athletes on that side of the ball who can range from one side of the field to the other, equally adept at coming up making tackles or covering wide receivers 40 yards down the field.

The Packers have had their share of quality safeties, but only a select handful could find a way to crack this All-Star roster. One is in the Pro Football Hall of Fame and the other probably should be. A fourth, who didn't make the cut, may well have taken his place as the best ever, but an injury cut his career short.

In their own way, each helped redefine the safety position and bring it into the forefront of the NFL.

BOBBY DILLON
All these years later, and with all the evolution of the pro game that has made passing the football central to its essence, it would seem logical that the guy who retired nearly six decades

ago would have given up his title as the Packers interception leader.

After all, there have been a lot more opportunities to pick off passes than there were in the 1950s, when Bobby Dillon patrolled the outer regions of the Packers defense.

But not so.

Bobby Dillon's 52 interceptions still remain the most in team history (Willie Wood is second with 48).

In his eight seasons with the Packers, Dillon never had fewer than four interceptions a season, and his low mark of four came in his rookie season, when he was a third-round draft pick. He led the Packers in interceptions in his first seven seasons and, remember, those were 12-game campaigns.

"Dillon is one of the few men in the league who can get the ball even when it's thrown perfectly," said Lisle Blackbourn, who was the Packers' head coach from 1954 to 1957. "He has that something extra."

And he needed it because Dillon played for some of the worst teams in Packers history. His first seven seasons, the Packers were a combined 26-54-2 and he went through four coaches.

His fifth coach, Vince Lombardi, immediately saw the value of Dillon and labeled him as one of the few untouchable players on a still developing roster.

But in June 1959, before Lombardi had coached a game, Dillon informed the new coach he was planning to retire to pursue a business opportunity in his native Texas.

Lombardi was stunned and, after saying that Dillon was irreplaceable "at this time," convinced him to come back for another season. But a leg injury sidelined him halfway through and he lost his starting job. He retired again and this time it was for good. He was only 29 years old but he'd had enough.

Dillon's 52 career interceptions, which still rank among the top 40 in NFL history, were impressive enough. What was even more amazing was that he did it with one eye.

Due to two accidents at age 10, he lost his left eye (it was replaced with a glass eye), but it never seemed to interfere with his play. In fact, some teammates never even knew he had a glass eye.

After football Dillon did some coaching and then went into business. He still lives in Texas. He was a four-time All-Pro and a four-time Pro Bowler, and in 2011 he was named to the Professional Football Researchers Association Hall of Very Good. He was inducted into the Packers Hall of Fame in 1974.

LeRoy Butler

Fair or not, for a new generation of Packers fans, when the name LeRoy Butler comes up, they think of the Lambeau Leap. He was, of course, so much more than that but, then again, sometimes perception is reality.

You remember. Right?

It was a frozen December Sunday afternoon at Lambeau Field in 1993 against the Los Angeles Raiders, who wanted to be anywhere else than where they were. A Packers rout was already on in the second half when a Raiders fumble was scooped up by Reggie White, who lateraled back to Butler, who took it down the sidelines for a touchdown.

However, Butler wasn't done.

"I don't know," he said after the game. "I just felt the need to jump in the stands and share it with the crowd. They went crazy."

And so what would become known as the "Lambeau Leap" was born. And ever since, it has become a staple of the Packers. Rookies and free agents, new to the Packers organization, can't wait to score a touchdown at Lambeau Field so they can do the leap. It has become another Lambeau tradition that can now be found at other stadiums around the league.

Butler enjoyed the notoriety of the invention for a while, but he also knew that he provided far more to the Packers of the 1990s than just a gimmicky jump into the stands.

A second-round pick from Florida State in 1990, Butler was the other Seminoles cornerback across from the more high-profile Deion Sanders. But there were many scouts who thought Butler had a bigger upside as a pro.

And after spending his rookie season as a cornerback, Butler was moved to safety, where he helped revolutionize the position.

It really began in 1994 when Fritz Shurmur became defensive coordinator. He saw Butler as a unique talent who could do more than just cover receivers and make tackles. He saw him as another pass rusher who could come from anywhere on the field, usually on a delayed blitz that would confuse offensive linemen and rival quarterbacks.

And in a four-year period, from 1995 to 1998, Butler put together the kind of seasons safeties rarely see. In that time he posted 381 tackles, 14½ quarterback sacks, and 18 interceptions as the Packers went to three NFC Championship Games and two Super Bowls (winning one).

In his 12 seasons with the Packers, Butler also became the most audible voice of the team, happily taking time for interviews and, often, saying things that would make his coach cringe.

For example, in training camp of 1997, the season after the Packers won Super Bowl XXXI, Butler boldly said that not only were the '97 Packers better, but there was a very good chance they'd go undefeated.

When the Packers lost their second game of the season, Butler stood before the media and said, "Why are you guys talking to me? I'm the dumb SOB who said we'd go undefeated. What do I know?"

That was Butler.

From brash rookie to NFL star to venerable statesman who helped train younger players, Butler did it all in his 12 seasons with the Packers. He played in 181 games, intercepted 38 passes, posted 20½ sacks, and registered 721 solo tackles. A four-time Pro Bowler and four-time All-Pro, he was also the first safety to record 20 sacks and 20 interceptions in a career. He retired after the 2001 season, having suffered a broken shoulder blade during the campaign.

Butler has remained in Wisconsin, working with different foundations, and he is featured on many radio/TV/social media outlets. Even in retirement, he still has plenty of opinions.

A finalist for induction into the Pro Football Hall of Fame, he is still waiting for the call, though few doubt he will one day gain entrance. He was inducted into the Packers Hall of Fame in 2007.

WILLIE WOOD

Undrafted, Unneeded. Unnecessary. That was Willie Wood in 1960. A running quarterback at the University of Southern California, the first African American quarterback at the school, Wood was told that no NFL team felt it needed his particular skill set. But, really, none of them wanted the headache of bringing a black quarterback into the NFL in the 1960s.

Undaunted, Wood wrote a letter to every NFL team seeking only a tryout, an opportunity to show teams what he could do. Only one team, Vince Lombardi's Packers, responded and offered him a tryout.

He was brought in with the other quarterbacks but Wood understood quickly he would never compete there. So he suggested a switch to safety and the rest, as has been said so often, is history.

"Determination was probably my trademark," Wood said during his 1989 speech at his induction into the Pro Football Hall of Fame. "I was talented, but so were a lot of other people. I'd like people to tell you I was the toughest guy they ever played against."

Wood anchored the free safety position for the Packers from 1960 until his retirement in 1971. He was a part of five championships in Green Bay and he set the tone for a defense that was considered the best in football.

"What a ferocious tackler he was," said fellow safety Tom Brown years later. "He didn't wrap his arms around people, he came in and dove at your legs and flipped you over a couple of times."

Wood's mark of 48 interceptions is still second all-time in team history (he led the NFL with nine in 1962) and his skills as a punt returner were almost as important as his work in the secondary. He scored two touchdowns on punt returns in 1961, led the NFL in punt return yardage in 1964, and remained the team's main punt returner his entire career, finishing with 187 returns.

"There wasn't anything he couldn't do," Lombardi said.

He would go on to earn seven trips to the Pro Bowl and five All-Pro nods and was inducted into the Pro Football Hall of Fame in 1989. He was also inducted into the Packers Hall of Fame in 1977.

Football took its toll on Wood, however, as for the past 10 years he's lived with dementia and, according to reports, has forgotten just about everything regarding his fabled career.

But Packers fans never will.

And the Winners Are . . .

Of all the positions, this is the toughest to limit to two. There are three great players on this list—and, in truth, Nick Collins should probably be among the candidates but misses out simply because of his length of service. Had he not suffered a career-ending neck injury, he may have surpassed everyone else.

So we're left to decide between Willie Wood, who was a defensive juggernaut of five NFL championship teams; LeRoy Butler, the heart and soul of the Packers teams in the '90s who redefined the free safety position; and Bobby Dillon, the team's all-time interceptions leader.

In the closest of close races, the winners are **Willie Wood** and **LeRoy Butler**. Try to complete anything deep on these two.

Safeties Who Did Not Make the Cut

What **Chuck Cecil** lacked in physical skill he made up for by simply being . . . physical. He was one of the hardest-hitting players the Packers have ever had and he'd hit anything that was moving. He was a fourth-round draft pick in 1988 and he immediately set a tone that if anyone planned to enter his sphere of influence, he would make him pay. For five seasons he was the face of Green Bay's defense and his thunderous tackles sometimes crossed the line between aggressive and dirty. But Cecil never cared. In 1992 he intercepted four passes and recorded 102 tackles to earn a spot in the Pro Bowl. For his Packers career, he recorded 340 tackles and intercepted 13 passes. He went on to play for the Phoenix Cardinals and Houston Oilers, then settled into defensive coaching with the Tennessee Titans and the Los Angeles Rams. In 2017 he returned to his alma mater, the University of Arizona, as a defensive analyst.

One of the more inspiring stories of a player overcoming the odds to enjoy a great career is **Mark Murphy**. An undrafted free agent out of tiny West Liberty College in West Virginia in 1980, Murphy hung on with grit and determination and the undying belief that his best would always be good enough. As a result, he went on to a solid 12-year career that included 20 pass interceptions and 11 quarterback sacks. But, as has been the refrain for many, he played on some teams that were simply not very good. Still, from where he came from to what he attained, it was a trip worth making. He was inducted into the Packers Hall of Fame in 1998.

Nick Collins could have been one of the greats in Packers history but, as is often the case, injury stepped in to derail a potential Hall of Fame career. Collins played for the Packers from 2006 to 2011, made three Pro Bowls, and intercepted 22 passes in 102 games, including one for a touchdown in Super Bowl XLV in February 2011. "Nick was a once-in-a-generation player with incredible range, speed, and ball skills," Packers quarterback Aaron Rodgers once said. But in a game on September 18, 2011, Collins collided with Carolina Panthers running back Jonathan Stewart and suffered a severe neck injury. He underwent spinal surgery that was successful, but the Packers were uncomfortable with letting him play again and released him in 2012. Collins continued to petition to play again, claiming he was healthy, but the NFL would not allow it. It has only been in recent years that he has come to grips with the fact he will not play again. His future was bright and his career was very good. But he still wonders what might have been. He was inducted into the Packers Hall of Fame in 2016.

PUNTER

The Candidates

Craig Hentrich
Tim Masthay
Josh Bidwell

They have their place, these guys who can be on the field 10 times a game or once.

There have been great punters in the NFL—guys with legs so strong and accurate they could change the course of a game and, in so doing, even change the course of a season.

Washington Redskins Hall of Fame quarterback Sammy Baugh was perhaps the game's first great punter, averaging more than 45 yards a kick in 13 seasons.

More recently, the Oakland Raiders' Ray Guy was the punter who was a cut above everyone. He was so good, for so long, that in 2000 the Ray Guy Award was established, honoring the top punter in college football.

He was a seven-time Pro Bowler, six-time All-Pro, a member of the NFL's 75th Anniversary Team and 1970s All-Decade Team, and the first punter elected to the Pro Football Hall of Fame. His dominance in the 1970s was crucial at a time before the NFL became the serial circus it is today.

In those days field position was everything, especially since teams still relied more on the running game than gobbling up huge chunks of yardage by throwing the ball.

Field position was still a science then, as coaches understood that by pushing the opponent deeper into its own territory with each possession, the offense would eventually benefit by having a shorter field to navigate.

And no one was better at changing those numbers than Ray Guy.

Then there are the Green Bay Packers, a franchise with Hall of Fame talent everywhere—except at punter. For the Packers it has never been a position that has unveiled epic, unforgettable talent.

To be fair, kicking footballs in Green Bay, Wisconsin, has always been a dicey prospect. For two months of the season it's not much of an issue, but October turns into November and the wind sweeps in off the bay, the temperatures plummet, the snow tends to fly, and kicking a football is not unlike trying to kick a cinder block.

Those kickers who step onto Lambeau Field at those times claim they love the challenge, and maybe they do. But, soon enough, they learn that kicking in Green Bay requires a certain fortitude and skill that not every kicker is up to.

So perhaps that's why punters in Green Bay will never win any league titles. More often than not, they will settle—reluctantly but realistically—for handling their jobs capably and conducting their duties without any discernible problems. Their job, often, is to keep the Packers out of danger and use to their advantage what the weather gives them.

It's not game-changing but it can be game-saving, and when you're kicking in an unforgiving environment like Green Bay, maybe that's enough.

So we introduce three punters who have done their best under sometimes trying circumstances. It may not be glamorous, but it is a living.

CRAIG HENTRICH

He could well have been an all-timer for the Packers, a guy destined for the Hall of Fame and a true difference-maker for the franchise—if he had stuck around longer.

An eighth-round draft pick of the New York Jets in 1993, he was picked up by the Packers late in 1993, still early in the regime of Ron Wolf and Mike Holmgren as they were putting their Super Bowl unit into place.

In 1994 Hentrich took over the punting duties from Bryan Wagner, who had kicked respectably in the previous season and a half.

Then, for the next four seasons, Hentrich was a mainstay on the Packers' powerful and decisive special teams. He averaged nearly 43 yards a punt and was the holder for two place-kickers, first Chris Jacke and then Ryan Longwell. And, when called upon, he could also kick extra points (he made all five he attempted) and field goals (he made three of five).

Hentrich had become one of those players the Packers organization and fans relied on when the time came to give the ball back to the other team.

He was part of the Packers' back-to-back Super Bowl appearances, steady and solid and, like the sunrise, expected to show up every day.

But after the 1997 season, when a flurry of Packers free agents were due to be dealt with, Wolf miscalculated. He expected it would not be problem to re-sign Hentrich, a player he had rescued from obscurity four years earlier.

Instead, Hentrich signed with the Tennessee Titans, and for the next 12 seasons he remained one of the game's most reliable and consistent punters.

It was one of the few missteps by Wolf, who admitted he was stunned by Hentrich's decision. And it cost the Packers over the next few seasons.

Indeed, over the next decade, the Packers had a veritable revolving door of punters—from Sean Landeta to Louis Aguiar to Josh Bidwell to Bryan Barker to B. J. Sander to Jon Ryan to Jeremy Kapinos to Tim Masthay to Jake Schum.

Meanwhile, Hentrich would take his place as one of the most respected Titan players in history, retiring after the 2010 season with a 42.9-yard punting average.

Tim Masthay

Red hair blazing with a pair of sideburns that could have had their own zip code, Tim Masthay was nicknamed "the Ginger Wolverine" by Packers teammates.

And he was also a pretty good punter.

Masthay was one of those punters who was part of the conveyor belt of kickers who came through after the loss of Craig Hentrich in free agency.

He had kicked collegiately for the University of Kentucky and went undrafted in 2009 before signing as a free agent with the Indianapolis Colts. He was released during training camp and remained out of football until the Packers signed him in the winter before the 2010 season.

He went on to punt for the Packers for the next six seasons, the longest tenure for a Packers punter since Don Bracken, who kicked from 1985 to 1990.

In 2011 Masthay set a franchise record for gross punting average (45.6 yards) and net punting average (38.6 yards), and in 2012 he threw a touchdown pass to Tom Crabtree in a win over the Chicago Bears.

In his six years with the Packers he averaged 44.2 yards a punt, but the Packers weren't thrilled with the lack of height he was getting on his punts and, in a surprise move, the team cut him in training camp in 2016, giving the job to Jake Schum, who lasted one season.

Masthay has been out of football since and now coaches college soccer in Kentucky.

JOSH BIDWELL

It is a rare, and often questioned, move for an NFL team to use a valuable pick in the annual draft on a punter. With all the needs teams have, using one of those selections for a punter is rather like buying a car to take out the garbage. Doesn't make a lot of sense—usually.

But in 1999 the Green Bay Packers not only used a draft pick on a punter, they used a fourth-round selection for University of Oregon punter Josh Bidwell.

From the strict perspective of value and contribution (which, frankly, is how drafts should be rated), the '99 draft was one of the weakest in the Ron Wolf regime.

Always able to find a so-called diamond in the rough, Wolf did not disappoint, plucking an unknown receiver named Donald Driver in the seventh round, a guy who would go on to become the team's all-time reception leader.

But the other 11 picks resulted in relatively little, except for third-round cornerback Mike McKenzie, who had a nice run in Green Bay before moving on in free agency.

Bidwell was one of Green Bay's two fourth-rounders, along with University of Virginia quarterback Aaron Brooks, who had no shot of playing since he backed up Brett Favre.

Yet punting was targeted as a need in 1999, as the Packers had struggled to fill the hole left two years earlier by the loss of Craig Hentrich. Veteran Sean Landeta, well past his prime, filled in for one season but Wolf knew he needed a longer-term option than that. So he rolled the dice and took Bidwell, the earliest he had ever taken a punter in a draft before.

And it appeared to be a decision that would work out, as Bidwell kicked well in training camp. But a week before the start of the season he was diagnosed with testicular cancer, which would require surgery.

He was placed on injured reserve and lost for the season, forcing the Packers into another stopgap measure. Tryouts led to the signing of Louis Aguiar, an eight-year veteran who had previously punted for the New York Jets and Kansas City Chiefs.

Aguiar's results that season were less than overwhelming, and when the following season rolled around, Bidwell, now fully recovered, beat out Tommy Hutton for the punting job.

He held the position for four seasons, averaging a credible 41.1 yards per kick and, at least for a while, allowing the Packers to focus on other areas of need.

But in March 2003 free agency again took a Packers punter as Bidwell signed with the Tampa Bay Buccaneers. A year later he earned his first (and only) Pro Bowl berth, and he was also named All-Pro.

Bidwell kicked five seasons with the Bucs, then moved on for one year with the Washington Redskins, where injuries cut short his season. He was released prior to the start of the 2011 campaign.

AND THE WINNER IS . . .

Not an easy choice for a position that is so subjective. But for the reaction of the Packers front office and the resulting difficulties in finding a long-term answer, the choice here is **Craig Hentrich**. A native of the Chicago area who played collegiately at Notre Dame, Hentrich knew all about the Packers mystique but, more important, he learned how to kick in lousy weather. And for four seasons he was one of the best in the business. Since his departure after the 1997 season, the Packers have gone through 10 punters, and the search continues. In 2018 the Packers drafted JK Scott from the University of Alabama in the fifth round.

PUNTERS WHO DID NOT MAKE THE CUT

Perhaps the most physically gifted punter the Packers have had in recent years was **Jon Ryan**, a Canadian who punted in 2006–07. In those two seasons he averaged nearly 46 yards a punt, but his days were numbered when he had two kicks blocked in the same game by the Chicago Bears. He was released after the 2007 season and then went on to kick for 10 seasons with the Seattle Seahawks. He was released prior to the 2018 season, signed with Buffalo, and then was released by the Bills, too.

And for sheer grit, let's give an honorable mention to **Don Chandler**, who punted and kicked field goals for the Packers for three seasons, from 1965 to 1967, after nine strong seasons with the New York Giants. In his three seasons in Green Bay, he averaged 42 yards a punt and made 58 percent of his field goals (48 of 83)—which in those days wasn't bad. But mostly he gets a nod for kicking in the 1967 "Ice Bowl." He punted eight times and averaged 29 yards a kick on a frozen field, with a rock-hard ball, and in temperatures dipping to near minus-20 degrees. He also kicked three extra points, which, again, was no bargain.

AFTERWORD

by Jerry Kramer

I have been involved with the Green Bay Packers organization for more than 60 years. When I say that out loud, it's almost impossible to believe, but there it is. I came to the Packers as a green, naïve kid, a fourth-round draft pick [out of the University of Idaho] in 1958 for a team that was the worst in the NFL. And ever since, I have remained close to this remarkable franchise, experiencing the kind of incredible times a kid from a small town in Montana never had a right to expect.

And over the decades—playing in memorable games involving unforgettable teammates and coaches—being a part of the Green Bay Packers has made me what I am and, perhaps more important, who I am.

I think about that often. I thought I'd probably be remembered for a couple of years after I retired and go back to Idaho and go into the logging business and drift off into the mists of time. Because, generally, linemen don't get remembered. It's stunning, really, because my beginnings were pretty modest and coming from a town of 252 people, just going to college was a huge thrill for me. That was the biggest thing that had happened in my life.

So it almost seemed like fate that things happened the way they did with me ending up with the Packers. It's like someone else was in control. I remember I received nine letters from

NFL teams and they were all addressed to "Dear Player." But Jerry Vainisi, the Packers personnel guy at the time, had a sawmill supervisor from Potlatch, Idaho, which is a few miles down the road from where I went to college, scout me. So the only guy who scouted me was the head of a sawmill.

I remember my college coach told me I wouldn't make the Packers team. It wasn't a maybe, it was, you're not going to make the team because they had five returning guards. But he told me not to worry about it, that I'd probably just be traded and I could play for somebody in the NFL.

So when I got to Green Bay, I was just waiting to be traded. I remember [head coach] Scooter McLean called me over after one practice and said, "What's the matter with you? You're looking over the fences and not paying attention." I said, "I'm waiting to be traded." And he said, "I didn't get you to trade you. Get with it, you're starting Friday night."

They traded two of those guards who ended up starting for the New York Giants and then in 1959 Vince Lombardi came along and changed my life. He was extremely important for me. He chewed my ass unmercifully on the field. I remember one practice in training camp, I missed a block and an assignment and he came running across the field and he came up to my nose and screamed, "College kids have an attention span of five minutes, high school is three minutes, elementary kids are one minute and kindergartners have 30 seconds. So where does that put you?"

This was like my second season with Lombardi and I thought, I'm never going to be able to play for this guy. Maybe it was time to do something else. I told this story often [including earlier in this book] but it has stayed with me forever and it's important. I was sitting in the locker room after that practice for maybe 40 minutes. I was lower than quail s---. But

Lombardi came over, rubbed my head, slapped me on the back and said, "Son, one of these days you're going to be one of the best guards in football." And an incredible warmth came into my chest. It was like a conversion. If he could believe in me, I could believe in me. I decided I'm going to give it everything I can to be the best and that's the first time it occurred to me. It was an incredible moment for me. It impacted my life. It impacted damn near everything I did.

He worked us so hard, but I was not impressed with him when I first saw him. But I remember there was a scout from the St. Louis Cardinals at one of our practices and he said, "I've been in the NFL for 25 years and I've never seen guys worked as hard as you guys are. If we did this in St. Louis, half the guys would be dead and half would quit." But that's what made him special. There was an energy source there I had never experienced before. It wasn't physical and it wasn't mental. It was emotional.

I remember when I first threw in with Lombardi. It was the championship game against Philly in 1960 [the Packers lost 17-13 and were stopped just yards from a winning touchdown when time ran out]. It was so frustrating to be that close, knowing you could run the ball and knowing you could score. I remember Coach didn't come into the locker room for maybe 15 minutes after the game. He finally comes in and he gets on a trunk and he says, "This year, we played in the championship; next year, we win the championship game." And I'm thinking, "By God he's right." If we play with what he preaches—consistency and discipline— we will. I threw in with him 100 percent at that point. And after that we were dominating teams. We believed in ourselves. We knew we were good and we should be good.

Those guys I played with, they were special. Every one of them believed in what we were doing. There are fewer and fewer of us these days and just in the last few months Forrest Gregg, Jim Taylor and, of course, Bart Starr have left us. I miss those guys.

I remember I didn't really believe Bart had what it took to be a great quarterback when he first came in the league. But he proved me wrong. I always thought we could win when he was quarterback. He had that ability to make everyone believe in him.

Those Packers teams helped change the NFL. They came around at the perfect time in this country. Pro football was really gaining popularity and the Packers were the kind of team America grew to love—or at least admire. A bit of it is the size of the city. It's the smallest city in the NFL by a significant margin. But this small city was able to overcome the New York Giants and Los Angeles Rams and Dallas Cowboys. And Coach Lombardi established a set of ethics that a lot of people followed: You don't do things right once in a while, you do it all the time. That made a difference with a lot of people.

And Green Bay fans, they're absolutely the top fans in the world. I remember my last game in Green Bay [in 1968]. We're playing Baltimore and we're down 16–3 with like four and a half minutes to go. And we start moving the ball right down the field and then we fumbled. It's a minute and ten seconds left to play and I walk off the field and I say, "It's all over. We're done. We're not going to the playoffs. An era is over." I come off the field and there is a smattering of applause from the crowd and I'm thinking, "It's over, we lost." But more and more people stand up and gave us a five-minute standing ovation. And then I thought, "They know it's over and they understand." It was a thank-you for so many wonderful years. That impressed me. It made me understand Packers fans a lot better. Their intelligence, their understanding of the game. It's pretty special.

It's been more than 60 years since I first stepped on the field in Green Bay. In some ways it feels like just yesterday. I guess I've evolved into something of a professional Packer over the years and I've been happy to do it. Whether it's a conference or a golf tournament or a fishing outing, Packers fans who weren't even alive when I played want to hear about the old days. There's still something special about those teams from so long ago that resonates with fans.

And as much as I enjoy talking about it, it's the present and the future of the Packers that matter most. I enjoy mingling with the new players each year and I watch as they learn and understand the history of a franchise that, very likely, will never be seen again. I also know that as long as there are fans like those in Green Bay and a commitment to excellence, the Packers will always command a special place in the NFL.

I was so lucky to play when I did and for the team I played with. I played with giants and I was coached by a legend and I hope that I have been able to provide a glimpse of just what that was like. Being a Green Bay Packer has been the highlight of my life and, every day, I realize how special that is.

Jerry Kramer played for the Green Bay Packers from 1958 to 1968 and was a member of five NFL Championship teams. He was a five-time All-Pro and three-time Pro Bowler, a member of the NFL 1960s All-Decade Team and was inducted into the Packers Hall of Fame in 1975. Long considered one the greatest players to never earn a spot in the Pro Football Hall of Fame, Kramer finally won induction in 2018 through the Seniors Committee. With his induction, there are now 25 Packers (including coach Vince Lombardi and general manager Ron Wolf) in the Hall of Fame.

THE GREEN BAY PACKERS ALL-TIME ALL-STAR TEAM

Head coach: Vince Lombardi

OFFENSE

Quarterback: Aaron Rodgers

Fullback: Jim Taylor

Halfback: Ahman Green

Tackles: Forrest Gregg, David Bakhtiari

Guards: Jerry Kramer, Gale Gillingham

Center: Jim Ringo

Tight end: Paul Coffman

Wide receivers: Sterling Sharpe, Don Hutson, James Lofton

Kicker: Ryan Longwell

Kick returner: Desmond Howard

DEFENSE

Defensive ends: Reggie White, Willie Davis

Defensive tackles: Henry Jordan, Cal Hubbard

Linebackers: Ray Nitschke, Dave Robinson, Clay Matthews

Cornerbacks: Herb Adderley, Charles Woodson

Safeties: Willie Wood, LeRoy Butler

Punter: Craig Hentrich

SOURCE NOTES

As any Green Bay Packers fan knows, there is no shortage of information regarding their favorite team. There are websites and books and magazines and newsletters that provide anything and everything that could possibly be needed when it comes to learning about the Packers, their players, and their history. And because of the specific nature of this book—in other words, selecting the best players at each position—I focused on some very specific source material to provide as much information as possible. Some of it is common knowledge to Packers fans but, hopefully, there's enough new material to raise the eyebrows of even the most die-hard fan.

In terms of online referencing, it was best to go straight to the ideal source, and that would be Packers.com and team historian Cliff Christl. His stories about players, especially the old-timers, were invaluable. Other websites I used include JSOnline.com and ESPN.com.

As far as other publications, I have used several of the books I've written on the Packers in the past. They include:

Game of My Life: Memorable Stories of Packers Football. Champaign, IL: Sports Publishing, 2004.
Green Bay Packers: Yesterday and Today. Lincolnwood, IL: Publications International, 2009.
Green Bay Packers: Where Have You Gone? New York: Sports Publishing, 2015.
Tales from the Green Bay Packers Sidelines. New York: Sports Publishing, 2015.
Facing the Green Bay Packers. New York: Sports Publishing, 2016.
Ice Bowl '67: The Packers, The Cowboys, and the Game That Changed the NFL. New York: Sports Publishing, 2017.

All other sourcing has been credited in the book when needed.

ACKNOWLEDGMENTS

This is the 12th book I've written on the Green Bay Packers, dating back to 1996. In that time, I have written about individual seasons, about Packers fans, and about players many fans will never forget as well as players who haven't been thought about in years.

For me it's been fun and educational, and I've enjoyed every syllable I've written on this unique franchise.

This project was a little different and easily the most subjective one I've written about the Packers. Creating an all-star team for a franchise featuring so many great players wasn't easy and over the course of writing this, I made many, many changes. But even in its final form, this team will not be greeted with universal acclamation, and that's fine. Disagreement makes life interesting, and I will let this work stand for itself.

I would like to thank Niels Aaboe at Lyons Press for the opportunity to write the book. As well, I'd like to thank my colleague at Albion College, John Perney, for editing the final draft and correcting the infuriating mistakes that seem to crop up when my brain writes faster than my fingers. And I'd like to thank the Green Bay Packers for their continued assistance. None of this happens without them.

So I hope you enjoy the final product. And whether you agree or not with the team that unfolds here, it's most important to remember the incredible wealth of talent this franchise has produced over the years in a little place like Green Bay, Wisconsin.

The Green Bay Packers saga remains an improbable story that, in another time and another place, probably never could have been written. But the great teams and players and seasons demonstrate that, 100 years later, it's a story that can never be forgotten.